Hildegard of Bingen

Mystical Writings

Hildegard of Bingen

Mystical Writings

✦ ✦ ✦

Edited by
Fiona Bowie and Oliver Davies

Translated by
Robert Carver

A Crossroad Book
The Crossroad Publishing Company
New York

This printing: 1999

The Crossroad Publishing Company
370 Lexington Avenue, New York, N.Y. 10017

Printed in the United States of America

Library of Congress Cataloging-in-Publication Data

Hildegard, Saint, 1098–1179.
    [Selections. English. 1990]
    Mystical writings / Hildegard of Bingen ; edited and introduced by
Fiona Bowie and Oliver Davies ; with new translations by Robert
Carver.
    p. cm. — (Spiritual classics)
    Includes bibliographical references.
    Includes discography.
    ISBN 0-8245-1027-5
    1. Mysticism—Early works to 1800.   2. Hildegard, Saint,
1098–1179. I. Bowie, Fiona. II. Davies, Oliver. III. Title.
IV. Series.
BV5080.H53213   1990
248.2'2—dc20   90-4789
                                                        CIP

To the Benedictine community of St Matthias
– formerly St Eucharius –
in Trier
with thanks
for their hospitality

O Euchari,
Valde beatus fuisti
cum Verbum Dei te in igne columba imbuit,
ubi tu quasi aurora illuminatus es,
et sic fundamentum ecclesie
edificasti.

O Eucharius!
You were blessed
When the Word of God seized you
In the dove's fire,
When, brilliant as the dawn,
You established your church.

HILDEGARD OF BINGEN

A Moment of Vision

I feel the air of another planet.
All the faces which just now were smiling
Have grown pale in the dark.

The well-loved trees and paths are fading
So I no longer know them and you, light
Lover shadow – the cause of my suffering –

Are smothered now in deeper fires, and appear
After the storm of raging frenzy
As an inward thrill of sensation.

Dissolved in sound, I circle, I weave,
In gratitude without end, praise without name,
And yield, undesiring, to the immensity of breath.

I shudder at the tempestuous airs
In the rapture of rites and shrill cries
Of supplicating women grovelling in the dust.

Then I watch and see translucent mists
Which rise in the clear sun-shot sky
And reach to the furthest mountain lairs.

The ground trembles white and soft as whey . . .
I soar aloft over gaping ravines
And sense how over the last cloud I swim

In a sea of crystal brilliance:
A spark of the sacred fire
A sound of the sacred voice.

STEFAN GEORGE

Contents

Illustrations

Preface

This anthology is intended to provide a general introduction to Hildegard of Bingen and her works for an English-speaking audience. The great interest in this remarkable twelfth-century prophet which has been manifest in Germany in recent years is now gradually spreading to other countries. It is not difficult to see why. First of all, Hildegard was a woman and, after centuries of neglect, the place of women in the history of spirituality and of the Church, as in all other areas of life, is now being reassessed. Secondly, Hildegard's message echoes many of our contemporary concerns. She has a holistic and ecologically sympathetic approach to life. She is interested in the feminine aspects of God, and has a rationalistic 'objective' view of human nature which is both integrated into her cosmology as a whole and modern in its approach and in many of its insights. Hildegard was also prodigiously talented and has attracted the attention of musicians, historians, theologians, literary critics and scientists, all of whom find much in Hildegard which is original and challenging.

Anthologizing works as varied and voluminous as those of Hildegard presents particular problems. Any selection in an anthology of this size could give a distorted view of Hildegard's work as a whole. The form of her visionary works, in which a vision is described and its significance developed over several pages, does not always lend itself to a shorter format. Then Hildegard's cosmological and medical schema permeates her works as a whole, and may not be easily grasped by looking at isolated passages. Having said this, however, we believe that the selection we have produced does succeed in giving the reader a taste of Hildegard's message, her range of interests, style, and personality. As the critical editions of

Hildegard's works appear, it is to be hoped that accurate English translations of her complete works will increasingly become available, following the lead of Barbara Newman's excellent edition of Hildegard's *Symphonia*.

In choosing passages we have been swayed by a number of factors; their intrinsic beauty and immediacy, their historical importance and their resonances for us today. Hildegard did not make clear distinctions between her visionary and scientific works. The whole of her life was inspired by and dedicated to God, and through her writings, Hildegard can remind us of the sanctity of all life. We therefore find similar themes, such as the importance of music to the spiritual life, appearing in her visionary works, in songs and in her letters. The effects of climate and of inheritance on personality may similarly be discussed in her spiritual exegesis, as well as in her medical and scientific works. The attempt to departmentalize and isolate different areas of our experience is foreign to Hildegard, and this comes through in her writings.

We would like to thank our translators, especially Robert Carver, for their patient and skilled work, and Peter Dronke and Cambridge University Press for permission to reprint extracts from *Women Writers of the Middle Ages* (1984). Our thanks too to Jean Williamson for drawing the map of Hildegard's world, to Huw Pryce for his comments on the manuscript, to Judith Longman of SPCK, to the sisters at St Hildegard's Abbey in Eibingen, and to all those who have shared with us their enthusiasm for Hildegard of Bingen.

Fiona Bowie
Oliver Davies
Bethesda, March 1990

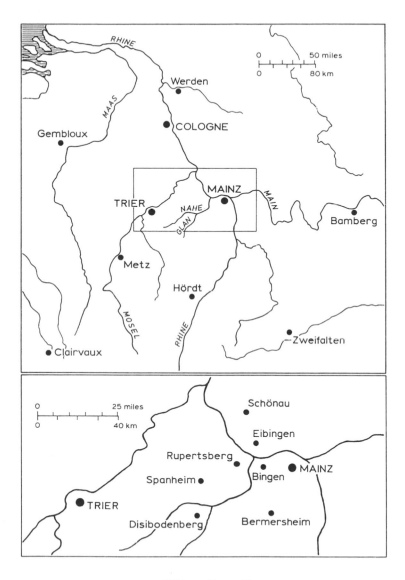

Hildegard's world

Abbreviations

SC	*Scivias*. References are to book, vision and chapter; e.g. *SC* I 4, 26 = *Scivias*, book I, vision 4, chapter 26
LM	*Liber vitae meritorum* (*Book of Life's Merits*)
DW	*Liber divinorum operum* (*Book of Divine Works*)
CC	*Causae et curae* (*Causes and Cures*)
B	Berlin Manuscript, Staatsbibl. Lat. Qu. 674
PL	*Patrologia Latina*, J. P. Migne
Pi	J. B. Pitra, *Analecta sacra*

PART 1

Introduction

A Time of Turmoil

Hildegard was born into a world in which everyone knew their place. There were those who ruled and fought, the kings, dukes, barons and their knights; those who prayed, the clergy, monks and nuns, and the mass of ordinary people who worked. Above all was God who had ordained this three-fold structure of society, and who had an interest in its maintenance. It would be another hundred years before the great movements for evangelical poverty swept across Western Europe and turned young noblemen into beggars. The Rule of St Benedict allowed for greater social equality, and the Cistercians, in a renewal of the primitive Benedictine Rule, engaged in manual labour, but on the whole religious communities mirrored wider social conventions. Hildegard and Jutta would have had a personal servant in their cell on the Disibodenberg, and in their Rupertsberg convent the aristocratic and high-born nuns were kept socially distinct from the low-born women who would have done much of the manual work in the community.

However stable the social hierarchy may have seemed, the political world was more uncertain. Although the danger of outside attack which had threatened the German Lands for centuries, with the Vikings to the north, the Saracens to the south and the Magyars to the east, had waned by the eleventh century, internally the country was torn by strife. Since the time of the great ninth-century emperor, Charlemagne, Germany had been ruled by semi-independent dukes, margraves and counts, often at war with one another and with the king. The Church was closely tied into the feudal system, its prelates receiving land and titles from secular rulers to whom they owed allegiance. Bishops were soldiers as well as clerics and both bishops and popes had their own armies which they would use to defend their titles and property, sometimes taking part in the fighting themselves.

During the eleventh century conflicting notions of religious and secular power began to develop. The monastic reform movement which had started at the Benedictine abbey of Cluny in Burgundy, and which led to the foundation of Disibodenberg in around 1105, had a profound affect on the Church as a whole. By the time Hildegard was born, in 1098, the papacy was no longer at the mercy of rival Roman patrician families, but it was locked in conflict with the German kings and emperors over their respective powers. A system had developed whereby the pope would anoint the German kings as Holy Roman Emperors, and the kings had a hand in the election of certain bishops and of the pope. To the reformers this dependence on secular power was unacceptable and both kings and popes fought for the right to invest bishops.

One of the best known of the eleventh-century reformist popes was Gregory VII, known as Hildebrand (1073–85). Before his election, Hildebrand had probably spent some time as a monk, possibly in a Cluniac monastery, as well as pursuing a distinguished career as a Vatican official. He sought to increase the mystique of personal sanctity surrounding the person of the pope as successor of Peter and as Christ's representative on earth. He claimed that all Christians were subject to the pope, including emperors, and that supreme judicial as well as spiritual power rightly belonged to the pope. As had his predecessors, Gregory VII attempted to stamp out clerical marriage and simony (the purchase of ecclesiastical office) and, more divisively, he tried to abolish royal control of bishops. This led him into direct conflict with the German king, Henry IV (1056–1106). Bishops were forced to choose between their feudal loyalties to the king and their spiritual loyalties to the pope, and in a series of shifting alliances various dukes and bishops attempted to play both parties off against one another to their own advantage. In 1076 Henry deposed Gregory, and Gregory responded by excommunicating Henry. As a political expedient Henry did penance to the pope the following year and the excommunication was lifted, but renewed in 1080 when Henry elected Archbishop Wibert

(Guibert) of Ravenna as antipope at an imperial council in Brixen. In 1084 Henry marched on Rome with his army in order to install Wibert as Pope Clement III, and to be crowned emperor by him. Pope Gregory VII took refuge in the St Antonio fortress before fleeing to Salerno where he later died.

What became known as the 'investiture controversy' rumbled on for many years under successive popes and German kings. A temporary peace was achieved between Henry V and Pope Callistus II at the Concordat of Worms in 1122. A formula was agreed whereby the emperor renounced the right to invest bishops with ring and crozier, the symbols of their spiritual authority, and to allow for their free canonical election and consecration. The emperor retained the right to be present at the election of bishops and abbots in Germany, a gesture towards their feudal allegiance to the crown. The uncompromising stance adopted by the only English pope, Hadrian IV (1154–9), angered the German emperor Frederick I, known as 'Barbarossa' ('red beard') by the Italians, and led to a further twenty years of strife and the election of a further three antipopes. Popes were by no means secure in their position. Innocent II (1130–42), who was elected on the same day as his rival, the antipope Anacletus II, spent most of his pontificate in France. Even the most saintly of the twelfth-century popes, the Cistercian monk Eugenius III (1145–53), who approved Hildegard's *Scivias* at the Synod of Trier, could not find a home in Rome, which was in the hands of the antipapal Roman commune. During her lifetime Hildegard saw some dozen popes and ten antipopes elected to the See of Peter. It was the age of the Crusades, with their idealism and barbarity, and it was a century marked by constant squabbles between local rulers and the German crown, between the crown and the papacy and between European royal families.

Hildegard's own sympathies would have been with the reformers in the Church, allied as they were to the monastic revival which gave life to her own community at Disibodenberg, and supported so strongly by her admired contemporary, Bernard of Clairvaux (1090–1153). Her interests were, however, by no means identical to that of the papacy and of the Church politicians. In a letter to the Archbishop of

Canterbury in 1102, Pope Paschal II expressed his disapproval of lay elections of bishops in the strongest possible terms:

> The honour of the Church is torn in pieces, the bonds of discipline are loosened and the Christian religion is dragged through the mud, if we allow the presumption of laymen to stretch out their hands to what we know to be the privilege of priests alone. It is not for laymen to betray the Church, nor for sons to stain their Mother with adultery.[1]

Superficially this is the language used by Hildegard in her frequently stated defence of the Church, but on closer inspection we realize that it is not the legal matter of lay investiture that occupied her mind, but the moral deportment of the Church's members. It is not laymen who despoil the Church through their election of bishops, but priests and bishops who are more concerned with their estates, their privileges and other secular matters than with ministering to their flocks.

Despite her respect for St Bernard, who was the driving force behind the Second Crusade (1145–9), Hildegard did not believe that those whose lives were dedicated to God should play the part of secular knights. In a vision of the Church she hears the common people complain, 'How can it be right that the shaven-headed with their robes and chasubles should have more soldiers and more weapons than we do? Surely too, it is inappropriate for a cleric to be a soldier and a soldier a cleric?' (DW 10, 16). The cleric and monk should set an example of piety, not of wealth, privilege and preoccupation with worldly concerns.

In Hildegard's world the Church and the state need one another. Spiritual power should suffice for the Church and secular power for the state. She never endorsed the more radical papal view of absolute supremacy, opting for the more modern notion of a balance and interdependence in the sharing of power so as to avoid abuses on both sides. This is perhaps why, although deploring his split with the papacy and his election of three antipopes, Hildegard continued to urge Frederick Barbarossa to fulfil his God-given mission as a Christian ruler.

Hildegard may have been a cloistered anchoress and an

enclosed nun, but she was by no means cut off from this turbulent world. Monasteries were part of the network of feudal ties and obligations. They were endowed by wealthy families who gave them land and goods in return for their prayers and spiritual works. Abbots and abbesses of large houses were powerful figures in their own right, commanding large incomes from their various estates and becoming major employers of labour. They were also respected figures, on an equal footing with their lay brothers and sisters who had remained 'in the world'. The heads of religious houses were not so unworldly themselves. Bernard of Clairvaux travelled widely and acted as advisor to several popes, while Hildegard left her convent to teach and preach throughout the Rhineland.

It is into this divided but vibrant world that Hildegard was born, and in which she lived out her mission. It was an age of expansion, geographically, with the Crusades pushing south and east; demographically, with the development of agriculture, towns and guilds; architecturally, with the foundation of numerous monasteries, great cathedral churches, castles and civic buildings; and of the mind, with the growth of universities, particularly the ancient medical school at Salerno, the law faculty in Bologna and the theological centre in Paris. From the lowliest to the most exalted in the land, Hildegard was in touch with the people who shaped her century and, like all great women and men, she both reflected and transcended her age.

Hildegard's Life and Works

HILDEGARD'S LIFE

The woman we know as Hildegard of Bingen was born in the year 1098 at a place called Bermersheim, near the town of Alzey in the beautiful German province of Rheinhessen.[2] The family appear to have been noble and well-connected. Hildegard's father, Hildebert, owned estates around Bermersheim in Rheinhessen, and was known to Count Stephan of Spanheim (or Sponheim), whose daughter Jutta founded the women's community at the Benedictine cloister of Disibodenberg. Two of Hildegard's brothers, Hugo and Roricus, were priests and one of her elder sisters, Clementia, became a nun at the Rupertsberg convent.

We possess little knowledge of Hildegard's early years, although she tells her biographer of an extraordinary gift which she possessed from her very earliest days. When she had scarcely learned to speak, Hildegard sought to convey to those around her something of the remarkable visionary life which was part of her nature and of which she wrote later that it had been imprinted on her while still in her mother's womb. It was this gift which was to shape her life dramatically from within, and it must have been strongly influential in her parents' decision to offer the eight-year-old Hildegard, their tenth child, as an oblate to the nearby Benedictine monastery of Disibodenberg.

Hildegard was put in the care of a young noblewoman, Jutta of Spanheim, who had rejected offers of marriage in favour of enclosure in an anchoress' cell (the life chosen by Julian of Norwich nearly three hundred years later). Jutta and the eight-year-old Hildegard, together with one or more servants, would have been walled up in a couple of small, spartan rooms. The formal religious service which marked their enclosure echoed the rites of burial. The women were to be hidden from the world, for the good of their souls and for the greater glory of God. Their cell was adjacent to the abbey church of Disibodenberg, the site of an earlier Celtic monastery which was refounded by Archbishop Ruthard of Mainz in around 1105 in the wake of the Cluniac Benedictine reforms. The first abbot was formally installed in 1108, two years after Hildegard's arrival on the site.[3] It is no wonder that Hildegard's later visions are so full of images of buildings and craftsmen, and that the construction of the Kingdom of heaven was seen as analogous to a human building project. The Disibodenberg monastery and its women's cloister were in a state of continual development throughout her forty-four years there.

Hildegard's early education would have been based on the liturgical requirements of a Benedictine abbey. She would have learnt to pray the Psalter in Latin and have heard, and later taken part in, the cycle of prayer and chanting which comprises the monastic life. Handcrafts were also recommended to keep the recluse from idleness, but more academic studies seem to have had no place in the anchorage. Hildegard later described Jutta as an unlearned woman, perhaps comparing her to the monks, who had greater access to books and to formal education.

As other young women came to join Jutta and Hildegard, so their accommodation expanded, and their life gradually changed from that of anchoresses to members of a Benedictine convent. When Hildegard was fifteen she took the habit of a Benedictine nun, and when Jutta died in 1136, Hildegard was elected as leader or *magistra* of the community. They remained dependent upon the monks for the services of a priest and in all financial and administrative matters. This restriction Hildegard came increasingly to resent, and as her reputation and confidence increased, she sought to remedy the situation.

An important figure in Hildegard's life was the provost of the convent, Volmar, who could not have been much older than Hildegard herself. Charged with special responsibility for the nuns' spiritual welfare, Volmar became one of Hildegard's closest friends and confidants, acting at times as a go-between between Hildegard and the abbot, and helping in the transcription of her visions. He continued in this role after Hildegard's move to the Rupertsberg in 1150, remaining with her until his death in 1173.

It was to Volmar that Hildegard turned when, in 1141,[4] she received the divine command to disclose the content of her visions. For many years Hildegard had told only Jutta of her strange gift, and Jutta in turn had alerted Volmar to her charge's secret. While Jutta was alive, however, Hildegard seems to have regarded her visions as more of a disability than a source of inspiration, accompanied as they were by debilitating illness. Now, as leader of her own community, a qualitative change seems to have taken place in Hildegard's personality. Although reluctant to reveal what she had seen and understood, the weakness of her youth was replaced by a new strength, both physical and spiritual. Volmar asked Hildegard to record her visions secretly so that he could assess their source, and then, recognizing their supernatural origin, he informed the abbot and began enthusiastically to assist Hildegard with their transcription.

There followed several years in which Hildegard worked on what became her first major visionary work, *Scivias*, a truly remarkable work, in which the most profound areas of the Christian revelation are represented in visionary form. She was aided by Volmar and a nun to whom she was particularly attached, Richardis of Stade (a cousin of Jutta's). Hildegard felt herself to have a new understanding of 'the writings of the prophets, the Gospels, the works of other holy men, and those of certain philosophers', based not on human learning but on direct inspiration from 'the living light'. She also discovered her great musical gifts and 'brought forth songs with their melody, in praise of God and the saints, without being taught by anyone', a talent which she put to good use in enriching the liturgical life of her community.

The question of Hildegard's education and the source of her wide and varied learning has generated much discussion, particularly as Hildegard herself continually stressed the divine source of all her knowledge. Barbara Newman is surely right when she lays stress not on what Hildegard knew, but how she knew it.[5] As her reputation grew, Hildegard's confidence increased and she found that her mental capacities too were illuminated by a divine light. The lessons she had absorbed over the years took on a new and original meaning and Hildegard's creativity blossomed. Ironically, the lack of formal instruction she had received may have shielded Hildegard from the more misogynistic elements of contemporary literature. Heloise, a contemporary of Hildegard who entered monastic life as an adult after a brilliant academic career under the tutelage of her teacher and lover Peter Abelard, was far more keenly aware than Hildegard of women's supposed inferiority.[6]

It was not, however, without trepidation that Hildegard embarked on her public ministry. The support and affirmation of men whom she respected, and who held authority in the Church, was vital to her. In 1146 she wrote to Bernard of Clairvaux, a leading monastic figure in the Cistercian (Benedictine) reform movement, asking for confirmation of her vocation. Bernard replied favourably, assuring Hildegard that her visions were genuine. The support of so great a figure would have helped to create a favourable atmosphere for the reception of Hildegard's work at the Trier synod of 1147–8, presided over by the Cistercian pope, Eugenius III. News of this remarkable visionary had reached Eugenius both from Bernard and from Heinrich, Archbishop of Mainz, and he sent a delegation to the Disibodenberg in order to visit Hildegard and to obtain a copy of her writings. Eugenius was favourably impressed and authorized Hildegard 'in the name of Christ and St Peter to publish all that she had learned from the Holy Spirit'.

The monks on the Disibodenberg were, no doubt, proud of their protegée. The enhanced reputation of the monastery, the visitors, the prospect of endowments, new vocations to the women's cloister, and the dowries the women brought with them, were all to be welcomed. Now a respected figure in her own right, the cramped quarters and lack of independence granted her cloister led Hildegard to take a difficult but decisive step. In a vision, which followed a period of illness,

Hildegard was told to leave the Disibodenberg with her sisters to found a new community. Despite her claim that the entire proceedings were directed by God, Hildegard had also enlisted the support of the Archbishop of Mainz and the Marchioness of Stade, the mother of Richardis, who may have had a hand in prospecting for a suitable site. Abbot Kuno was at first unwilling to grant permission for the move, and neither the nuns themselves, nor their families, could see the necessity of leaving a place where they were comfortable, and which they had generously endowed. Reacting to criticism from local people that she was mad or possessed, Hildegard took to her bed and lay there immobile. When Kuno failed to lift her he became convinced that this was no ordinary illness, but a sign of divine disapproval. As soon as he relented, Hildegard rose from her bed, restored to health. Building work began on the new site and in 1150 Hildegard made the day's journey down the River Nahe to the Rupertsberg together with twenty of her sisters. As Sabina Flanagan has it, 'she had emerged from the shadow of the monastery of Disibodenberg into the sunlight of her own foundation'.[7]

The journey to full independence was not yet complete. In order to maintain a viable institution Hildegard needed to wrest control of the women's finances from the monks on the Disibodenberg, and she sought to establish a principle whereby the monks would supply the nuns with a provost of their choice to oversee their spiritual welfare. The early years on the Rupertsberg were ones of considerable hardship and poverty, and it was not until 1158 that Hildegard finally succeeded in obtaining a charter regulating the distribution of assets between the two houses. Her standing with the abbots of Disibodenberg and in the eyes of local families was by no means sufficient to ensure that she could get her own way, even when appealing to the authority of 'the living light'.

It is to this period that Hildegard's two scientific works belong: the *Natural History* (*Physica*) and the *Causes and Cures* (*Causae et curae*). The former is an ingenious study of the many aspects of the natural world, while the latter, which concentrates upon the working of the human body, is a medical compendium. Hildegard also wrote a second visionary work,

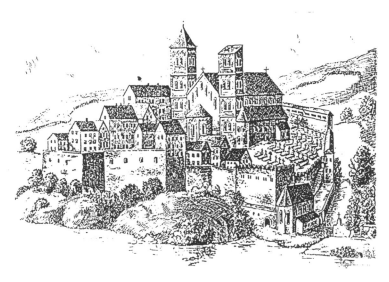

Rupertsberg in 1625

the <u>*Book of Life's Merits*</u> (*Liber vitae meritorum*), in these years which, according to remarks in her biography, may well reflect her concern with pastoral issues in the new convent. Here she describes both the vices and the virtues in brilliantly colourful and poetic imagery.

With the economic foundations and independence of her community assured, Hildegard was able to turn her energies in a new direction. In around 1158 a <u>prolonged illness</u>, the prelude to most of Hildegard's major decisions, was followed by her first preaching tour. Already around 60 years of age, the woman who had been enclosed for life as a child, and who had been <u>cloistered for over fifty years</u>, set out on a most unfeminine mission, to preach the Word of God in the towns and villages along the River Main. The words of Scripture recorded in 1 Timothy 2.12, which forbid a woman to teach in public, might be thought to preclude such a step, but Hildegard felt impelled by her inner voice and dared not refuse. Over the next twelve years, despite long periods of ill health, Hildegard made four such journeys within a radius of some 200 kilometres of Bingen, speaking both to clergy and to lay people, sometimes in the chapter houses of religious communities, and sometimes in public. Although she described herself as 'a simple creature' and as a 'poor little woman', Hildegard's writings and letters, some of which record the texts of her public sermons, display a remarkable assurance and originality. She felt confident enough to address the most exalted lay and religious leaders of her day, whilst never losing her interest in the ordinary workings of the human mind and body, or of the natural world around her.

In 1163, Hildegard began her third and final visionary work, the *Book of Divine Works* (*De operatione Dei*), in which in a series of visions she once again presents the theme of God and the creation. This is Hildegard's most accomplished work. Two years later she established a second foundation, at the former Augustinian double monastery across the Rhine at Eibingen, near Rüdesheim. She visited this new community twice a week, but experienced many pastoral problems with the nuns there, some of whom eventually returned to secular life

At the very end of Hildegard's life there occurred an event which throws a clear light on her uncompromising adherence to the truth of the gospel. It appears that Hildegard permitted a nobleman, who had been excommunicated, to be buried in the convent cemetery after he had been reconciled with the Church and had received the sacraments. Unaware of the circumstances, or unwilling to explore them, the Church authorities at Mainz imposed an interdict upon the community at Rupertsberg, which meant that Hildegard and her nuns were denied the sacraments and were hindered in their rhythm of praise. Despite Hildegard's carefully constructed protestations and the intervention of witnesses, the authorities failed to respond. It was only some while later, when Hildegard appealed directly to Archbishop Christian of Mainz, who was away in Rome, that the situation could be satisfactorily resolved.

Some seven months later, on 17 September 1179, Hildegard died peacefully and in the bosom of her community. Her canonization process, which was initiated not long after her death, was never formally completed due to administrative difficulties. But in 1324 Pope John XXII gave permission for her 'solemn and public cult', and Hildegard's status today is that of a canonical saint. Her feast is celebrated in the German calendar on the anniversary of her death.

HILDEGARD'S WORKS

Scivias, which means literally 'Know the Ways', is the first and the longest of Hildegard's visionary works (1141–51). It is divided into three sections or books, consisting of six, seven and thirteen visions respectively. Hildegard first records each vision in detail and then gives its theological explanation, which is presented by a 'voice from heaven'.

Book One begins with the theme of wisdom, which is human knowledge and inquiry illumined by faith, humility and revelation, and it progresses to the theme of humanity in the bondage of original sin. Then Hildegard turns to the creation, at the heart of which there stands an unredeemed humanity, to the old Covenant which anticipates the coming of Christ and to the angelic order with its promise of fulfilment to come.

Book Two presents the theme of the Saviour, the Church – its hierarchy and sacraments, particularly baptism, confirmation and the Eucharist – and the theme of continuing temptation and evil.

Book Three explores the work of the Holy Spirit in building up the Kingdom of God through the virtues, and the last visions of this book are concerned with the Day of Judgement and the New Earth. The final vision of all, the 'Play of Virtues' (*Ordo virtutum*), is dominated by the theme of victory and praise, and its blend of action and personification justify its description as the first morality play. Hildegard herself later developed the *Ordo* as an independent piece and set it to music.

The Book of Life's Merits (*Liber vitae meritorum*) is Hildegard's second visionary work (1158–63). It consists of six visions, each of which describes the figure of a man who looks towards different points of the compass, with a commentary. The first five visions present thirty-five pairs of virtues and vices, the latter of which are examined in fuller detail than the former, together with penances for their expiation and removal. The vices also appear in visible form (unlike the virtues), and Hildegard manages to present a powerful and expressive representation of purgatory and of hell. The final book turns to more general themes such as judgement and the promise for the blessed of glory in heaven.

The Book of Divine Works (*De operatione Dei*) is the third and final of Hildegard's visionary works (1163–73/4). This, too, is divided into three parts and, again like *Scivias*, it seeks to address the Christian mystery in its full cosmological depth. The work consists of ten visions of varying lengths, divided into three books which are themselves of different lengths. The first book, which consists of the first four visions, deals with God's creation of the world from love and with the special place of humanity within it. The second book, or fifth vision, develops the idea of humanity as the moral centre of the world, faced with ultimate divine judgement, while the third book, which consists of the last five visions, is concerned with salvation history, with the incarnation and the end of time. The central part of the work is Hildegard's long meditation on the opening of St John's Gospel, which forms a considerable section of the fourth vision.

The Book of Divine Works is a broad cosmological reflection on the Christian revelation from a profoundly anthropocentric point of view according to which men and women, who are themselves the 'work' of God, are called to co-operate actively with God in the perfection of his creation.

The Natural History (*Physica*) was written between 1151 and 1158. It describes the healing powers of plants, elements, trees, jewels, animals and metals, while giving an account of their origin. *Causes and Cures* (*Causae et curae*), which dates from the same period, is a medical compendium which addresses the constitution of the human body, its illnesses and their remedies. Both these books originally constituted a single work with the title *The Subtleties of the Diverse Nature of Created Things* (*Liber subtilitatum diversarum naturarum creaturarum*).

Hildegard was also the author of seventy-seven songs for which she herself composed the music. The language of these songs is particularly beautiful, and their accompaniment is strikingly original. The themes which they address range from the three Persons of the Trinity, to Mary, the angels, patriarchs and prophets, the apostles and martyrs, as well as individual saints. And some are songs written on the occasion of the dedication of a church. Hildegard's corpus of songs is known as the *Symphonia*, and it is believed that they were in greater part complete by the year 1158.

During her life time, Hildegard also wrote a good many letters, of which some three hundred survive. These give us valuable insight into her private thoughts and personal struggles, as well as her public mission to advise and, when necessary, to correct. Hildegard corresponded with a great variety of people, including four popes (Eugenius III, Anastasius IV, Hadrian IV, Alexander III), numerous local rulers (including the King of England, Henry II) and even the emperor (Barbarossa, or Frederick I, whom she actually met), numerous archbishops and bishops, abbots and abbesses, leading spiritual figures (Bernard of Clairvaux, Elisabeth of Schönau), many priests and lay people.

Hildegard's other works, which generally date from a later period, include a selection of readings from the Gospels, with an allegorical commentary (the *Expositiones evangeliorum*), commentaries on the Rule of St Benedict (*Explanatio Regulae S. Benedicti*) and on the Athanasian Creed (*Explanatio Symboli S. Athanasii*), and two biographies: the *Life of St Disibod* (*Vita Sancti Disibodi*) and the *Life of St Rupert* (*Vita Sancti Ruperti*). There is also the *Solutions to Thirty-Eight Questions* (*Solutiones triginta octo quaestionum*), in which Hildegard attempted to solve theological problems put to her by the monks of Villers and Guibert of Gembloux, and there are two short pieces entitled the *Unknown Language* (*Lingua ignota*) and the *Unknown Writing*

(*Litterae ignotae*). The former is a glossary of some nine hundred words which Hildegard herself created and which are arranged in thematic groups.

The Living Light

The role of visions in the experience of medieval women is analysed by Elizabeth Petroff in her perceptive introduction to her book *Medieval Women's Visionary Literature*:

> Visions led women to the acquisition of power in the world while affirming their knowledge of themselves as women. Visions were a socially sanctioned activity that freed a woman from conventional female roles by identifying her as a genuine religious figure. They brought her to the attention of others, giving her a public language she could use to teach and learn. Her visions gave her the strength to grow internally and to change the world, to build convents, found hospitals, preach, attack injustice and greed, even within the Church. Visions also provided her with the content for teaching although education had been denied her. She could be an exemplar for other women, and out of her own experience she could lead them to fuller self-development. Finally, visions allowed the medieval woman to be an artist, composing and refining her most profound experiences into a form that she could create and recreate for herself throughout her entire life.[8]

These words could have been written with Hildegard in mind, and they certainly apply to her. She founded two monasteries, at Rupertsberg and Eibingen. She certainly preached, composed, taught, reflected upon and utilized her visions in her work of healing and in the working out of her theology. They also gave rise to the extraordinary illustrations which accompany *Scivias* and *The Book of Divine Works*, the former almost certainly completed in the Rupertsberg scriptorium during Hildegard's lifetime, and the latter, utilizing a similar style, undertaken in the thirteenth century. What then were these visions? Their content is laid out and expounded in Hildegard's great visionary trilogy, but what interested so many of her contemporaries, as well as later inquirers, was the manner in which they came to her.

From autobiographical extracts in her _Vita_ we know that Hildegard 'saw so great a brightness that my soul trembled' when she was only three, that she discovered in herself the ability to foretell future events (such as the colour of a calf in its mother's womb), and that her normal perceptions were unaffected by her inner vision. It is in a letter written in response to the persistent requests of the Walloon monk, Guibert of Gembloux, that Hildegard gives the fullest account of her visions. It appears that the faculty to see things with her soul was constantly present, both by day and by night, and that this gift was immensely taxing to Hildegard's health. What she sees, Hildegard describes as a non-spatial light, which she termed 'the reflection (or shadow) of the living light'. This light would produce images, sometimes accompanied by a voice which addressed her in Latin, and which she claimed to record faithfully. Only on one occasion does Hildegard describe a vision which was accompanied by a loss of normal consciousness, and she interpreted this as a prelude to the writing of her third and most accomplished visionary work 'in which many investigations of the creations of the divine mystery would have to be pursued'.[9] The illustrations accompanying _Scivias_ and _The Book of Divine Works_ give us an inkling of what Hildegard saw in her visions, although they remain static, unable fully to portray the great dramas of colour, movement and sound, resonant with symbolic significance, which her writings describe.

Modern interest has followed the observations of Charles Singer, a medical historian, who saw in Hildegard's description of her visions evidence of migraines.[10] But Hildegard too was interested in the physiological basis of her visions. She described her temperament as 'airy', easily affected by changes in the weather and prone to infirmity. The four humours were unbalanced in her, producing a permanent vulnerability, but also enabling her to become the dwelling place of the Holy Spirit, perceived as a spiritual wind to which her soul was especially sensitive. Her visions, the presence of the 'living light' and her poor health were therefore intimately connected, and from an inherent weakness Hildegard learned to draw her strength.

Unlike the visions of her younger contemporary and friend, Elizabeth of Schönau, or those of other twelfth and thirteenth-century women mystics such as Marie of Oignies, Mechthild of Magdeburg or Hadewijch of Brabant, Hildegard's message was prophetic and didactic.[11] She has little in common with the intensely devotional, erotic and ecstatic mysticism of the beguine writers mentioned above, and her theology is theocentric or sapiential, rather than christocentric. It is the cosmic dimension, the struggle between good and evil, an absorption with the great work of redemption and the role of human beings in that work, which preoccupy Hildegard. She does not present herself as a role model or lay down a path of mystical union for others to follow. Hildegard is, rather, a mouthpiece, a 'small trumpet', a 'feather on the breath of God', whose task it is to teach and correct her fellow men and women and to glorify the Creator.

Hildegard claimed direct divine intervention as the source of all her visionary works, her music and many of her letters and pronouncements. One is, however, left with the impression that Hildegard could overstate her case, and that some of her contemporaries regarded her statements with a degree of scepticism. The claim that 'the divine light has spoken' and the invocation of terrible curses for those who ignored it, might on occasions have resembled the rantings of an old woman who had been thwarted, rather than a mouthpiece of God. An example of Hildegard's style can be seen in her *Vita*, in a passage describing her efforts to obtain independence for her convent from the monks at Disibodenberg. What Hildegard describes as a 'petition' was, as Peter Dronke so rightly points out, more of a 'fulmination'.

> And in accordance with what I perceived in my true vision, I said to the Father Abbot: 'The serene light says: You shall be father to our provost, and father of the salvation of the souls of the daughters of my mystic garden. But their alms do not belong to you or to your brothers – your cloister should be a refuge for these women. If you are determined to go on with your proposals, raging against us, you will be like the Amalekites, and like Antiochus, of whom it was

written that he despoiled the Temple of the Lord. If some of you, unworthy ones, said to yourselves: Let's take some of their freeholds away – then I WHO AM say: You are the worst of robbers. And if you try to take away the shepherd of spiritual medicine [i.e. Provost Volmar], then again I say, you are sons of Belial, and in this you do not look to the justice of God. So that same justice will destroy you.'[12]

In both her *Vita*, and at the end of each of her visionary works, Hildegard emphasizes their divine origins and warns against altering her words in any way, saying, for instance, in the *Book of Life's Merits*, 'Wherefore if anyone, through an overweening pride in his own writings and opinions, adds anything to them in contradiction, he is worthy to suffer the pains here described. Or if anyone removes anything from them through perversity, he is worthy to be removed from the joys here revealed.'[13] These protestations reveal the fragility of Hildegard's authority. As a woman she had no right to teach others, only as a mouthpiece of God could she appropriate this male and priestly prerogative. As Barbara Newman put it:

In these brazen confrontations with her readers, daring them to accept all or nothing, Hildegard betrays both more and less than total assurance. Texts such as these, interwoven as they are with references to her own simplicity, frailty and femininity, insist on her authority with a defiance proportional to her fear that her books would indeed be concealed, altered, abridged, ridiculed or ignored.[14]

It is to Hildegard's relationship with the living light, her extraordinary visionary gift, that we can attribute the transformation of 'a poor womanly creature' into the 'sybil of the Rhine'.

Hildegard's Theology

One of the major achievements of Hildegard of Bingen is that her work embraces the full breadth of the Christian revelation in a fresh and original way; and this fact alone puts her in a small group of outstanding doctors of the Church. Not content with concentrating on one or two specific aspects of the Christian life or revelation, Hildegard is concerned with the whole of creation, with the place of humanity, of sin and redemption. She thus creates a *cosmology* in the true sense of the word: a system which represents and explores the whole

And yet, at the same time, Hildegard was a teacher and her instincts were paramountly pastoral. This means to say that the cosmology which Hildegard presents is not a dispassionate attempt to investigate the origins of the universe; rather it is an inspired (and passionate!) attempt to represent the world in such a way that we, her audience, will better understand what it is that we must *do* in order to fulfil the divine plan and to express the fulness and the goodness of our own nature.[15] In other words, although many of the elements in Hildegard's teaching derive from earlier treatises on the nature of the universe, her handling of them is entirely new in that the very structures of the universe are taken up into a vision of the great cycle of creation, of sin and redemption, which has humanity at its centre. Nothing in Hildegard's work, despite its immense range, is untouched by her need to explore the primal drama of God, humanity and the Redeemer. There is therefore a dynamism, a brilliance and an urgency in her work which is all her own.[16]

A brief look at the very first vision of her first work (*Scivias*) can illustrate something of the way in which Hildegard proceeds (see illustration on page 25). At the very centre of this vision is the glory of God in his unapproachable and un-fathomable light; and yet this is not a remote glory but one which engages with us, protecting us and revealing to us 'the unutterable justice of final victory'. The remaining two figures in the vision both represent our proper response to the light. The first figure, which is covered with eyes, is the 'fear of God'. This is the principle of ever-watching alertness, the constant vigilance of the human spirit as it strains always to receive the energies and the light of God. The second figure is the necessary state of being which accompanies this tuning of the mind to God. This is the figure of a small girl who is 'poverty of spirit', and who reminds us that it is only deep humility and obedience to God which support and sustain the vision of his light. The vision concludes with the statement that all our actions, both good and bad, lie open to God's view and, while acknowledging that human action shows a mixture of 'luke-warmness and sincerity', Hildegard speaks of those who walk the 'path of truth' and urges us to take her warning to heart.

Here, as elsewhere, the source of Hildegard's inspiration is light, sublime light whose origin is within the Godhead itself. The radiance of the first vision tallies well with what Hildegard tells us elsewhere about the living, divine light, which she glimpses only upon occasion, and the 'reflection of the living light' which seems to be the medium of the visions themselves. In *Scivias*, in the first vision, both forms of light are present, one which is remote and impenetrable and the other which communicates itself as revelation.

But with the presence of the small girl who, representing poverty of spirit, stands before the throne of God and receives the divine light, Hildegard shows us the centrality of the human dimension in her vision.[17] The communication of the divine light takes place within a human space, and at no point does Hildegard wander from her primary intuition of the special and integral role of humanity within the creation. As we will see, she believes that the creation itself is indelibly marked with a human outline; just as humanity contains within itself elements of the universe as a whole.

Finally, Hildegard's remarks at the end of the vision remind us that her concern is paramountly didactic and pastoral. She

profunditatem expositionis libro-
ix sentiens. uiribusq; receptis de
dine me erigens uix opus istud
anni consummani ad finem
. In diebus autem HEINRICI
turi archiepi ⁊ Conradi roma
i regis ⁊ Cunonis abbatis in
beati DYSIBODI pontificis.
pa Eugenio he uisiones ⁊ uerba
unt. Et dixi ⁊ scpsi hec ⁊ secundu
ratione cordis mei aut ullius ho
sed ut ea in cęlestib; uidi audiui
p secreta misteria di Et iterum
uocem de cęlo michi dicentem.
⁊ scribe sic.

nt capitula libri scinas
ticis hominis
a piue uisionis piue partis
fortitudine ⁊ stabilitate ciuitati
ei.
e domini.
i paupes spu sunt.
rutes a do uenientes. timtes dm
s spu custodiunt.
ptioni di absconditi n possunt
rctuum homininm.
a de eadem re.

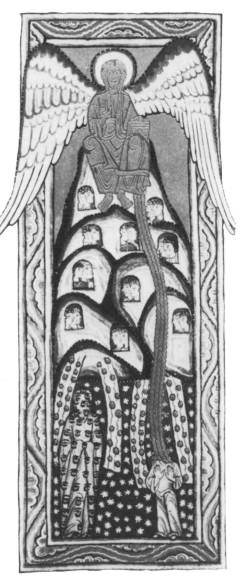

The Glory of God

wishes to instruct us in the ways of God, to point out the evils and dangers inherent in our fragile nature, and to urge us to 'walk the path of truth', which shall lead ultimately to bliss and salvation. And so, despite the sublimity of her revelations, Hildegard remains deeply orientated towards the needs and situation of her fellow human-beings.[18]

THE CREATION

The creation, for Hildegard, begins in the love of God, as this passage from the *Book of Divine Works* shows:

> The leaping fountain is clearly the purity of the living God. His radiance is reflected in it, and in that splendour, God embraces in his great love all things whose reflection appeared in the leaping fountain before he ordered them to come forth in their own shape. And in me, Love, all things are reflected and my splendour reveals the design of things, just as the reflection indicates their form. In Humility, who is my helper, creation has come forth at God's command; and in that same Humility, God has inclined himself towards me, to lift up again in that blessedness the withered leaves that have fallen and through whom he can do all that he will. For he fashioned, them out of the earth; and from the earth he freed them after the fall. (*DW* 8, 2)

In this passage it is striking that this same love of God, which contains all things in itself, contains humanity too, together with our fall into sin and our redemption from sin through the incarnation of his Son. Right from the very beginning therefore, Hildegard's creation is one which not only contains a foreknowledge of the great drama of the fall and our redemption, but finds in this its own essential *meaning*. And it is also significant that the 'voice' in this passage is that of the love of God, which is personified as a young woman. As Barbara Newman has shown, the 'eternal feminine, in her several guises, links God's coming into the world with the world's own coming to be'.[19] Hildegard's vision of the creation is profoundly christocentric therefore (with Christ at its centre) in that it is so deeply anthropocentric (with humanity at its centre). This is confirmed by another important passage in which the Love of God again speaks, which is the source of all life, and which tells us how it has 'kindled every living spark' and how it is aflame 'above the beauty of the fields', gleaming 'in the waters' and burning 'in the sun, the moon and the stars'. Yet again Hildegard quickly asserts the primacy of the human: 'For it was always the case throughout eternity that God wanted to create his work – man. And when he had finished this work, he gave all creatures to him so that with them he might work, just as God himself had made his work, which is man' (*DW* 1, 2). Likewise, in her vision of the great 'cosmic wheel' which supports all creation, Hildegard tells us that it is humanity which is at its centre: 'Humanity stands in the midst of the structure of the world. For it is more important than all other creatures which remain dependent on that world. Although small in stature, humanity is powerful in the power of its soul' (*DW* 2, 15). And, in another passage, Hildegard makes it clear that the fall of Adam and Eve has repercussions for the whole of the creation, for 'in their misfortune and their exile every creature in the world is shrouded in cloud, as when a ray from the sun shines through dense cloud' (*DW* 5, 15).

For Hildegard, the creation itself takes place through the Word of God. Here, of course, she is following the teaching at the beginning of the Gospel of St John ('through whom all things were made': John 1.3). Also, in a sense, created things remain *within* the Word.[20] Thus we read:

> The Word sounded and brought all creatures into being. In this way the Word and God are one. As the Word sounded, he called to himself all of creation which had been predestined and established in eternity. His resonance awakened everything to life, just as God had indicated within humanity. God secretly speaks the Word within his heart before God emits the Word. This is the Word which still remains within God, even though it is sent forth. Thus whatever is uttered by the Word remains in the Word. Now when the Word of God sounded, this Word appeared in every creature, and this sound was life in every creature. (*DW* 4, 105)

The dependence of the life of creation on the Word is an important idea for Hildegard, as it reinforces the image of a creation which is vibrant with divine life. Elsewhere, for instance, Hildegard tells us that 'the Son exists in such glory that every creature is illuminated by the brightness of the Word's light' (*SC* I 3, 4).

But despite the centrality of humankind in the overall plan of creation, Hildegard also has a vigorous sense of the transcendent *otherness* of creation. In a number of passages she speaks of the way in which creation is brilliant with divine life, and she states that it is creation which reveals to us the God who cannot be seen: 'God cannot be seen but is known through the divine creation, just as our body cannot be seen because of our clothing' (*DW* 9, 14). Creatures emerge from God as sparks: 'all the living sparks are rays of his splendour, just as the rays of the sun proceed from the sun itself. And how would God be known to be Life except through the living things which glorify him, since the things that praise his glory have proceeded from him?' (*DW* 4, 11). Above all, it is the sense of *life* in creatures which fascinates Hildegard, what she calls their 'radiance', which may be their 'greenness' or seeds or flowers or beauty' (*DW* 4, 11). And she roots this power fundamentally in the dynamic, vibrant life of God himself, who is the 'Life of all life' (*DW* 4, 105).[21]

HUMANITY

The core of Hildegard's understanding of the role of men and women within the creation can be found in a remark she makes in her *Life*: 'Humanity too is God's creation. But humanity alone is called to co-operate with God in the creation' (*Vita* II, 35).[22] That special role which we have within the created order and which emerges so clearly from Hildegard's discussions of the nature of the creation, is that we alone possess the power to fashion according to our own will those things and creatures which have been created by God. After all, we alone of all creatures possess reason, the light of discrimination (cf. *SC* III 2, 9), and so we can choose either to co-operate with the goodness of God, or to defy him and to oppose his order. This is Hildegard's central perception concerning humankind, and it is the one which gives such a keen edge to the didactic character of her work.

Even a cursory view of her writings will persuade us how intensely interested Hildegard is in the human phenomenon. She writes at length of each part of the human body and never tires of trying to explain its workings, according to her own understanding of the structure of the world of which we are a part. And indeed, she conceives of humanity very much as a *microcosm* of the world's *macrocosm*; for 'God fashioned the human form according to the constitution of the firmament and of all the other creatures, as the founder has a certain form according to which he makes his vessels' (*DW* 4, 97). Human beings are the 'complete creation of God' (*plenum opus Dei*) and we contain both the things of the earth and those of heaven: 'Thus humankind is earthly according to its humble station in the flesh and heavenly because of the heights of heaven which it possesses in its soul' (*DW* 4, 99). And Hildegard compares the soul directly with the moisture which gives life to the earth: 'The soul is the green life-force of the flesh. For, indeed, the body grows and progresses on account of the soul, just as the earth becomes fruitful through moisture. And the soul is also the moisture of the body because the soul moistens it so that it does not dry out, just as rain flows down into the earth' (*DW* 4, 21). In another example, she compares the proportions of the human head (the seat of the soul) with the harmony of the created world: 'The sphere of the human head indicates the roundness of the firmament, and the right and balanced measurements of our head reflect the right and balanced measurement of the firmament' (*DW* 4, 16). And in a further passage, Hildegard argues that we are ourselves constituted by the very same elements which make up the external world:

> As has already been shown a number of times, just as the four elements hold the world together, they also form the structure for the human body. Their distribution and function in the whole human being are such that they constantly sustain the person, just as they are spread throughout all the rest of the world and have their effects. Fire, air, water and earth are in humankind, and humans consist of them. From fire they have the warmth of their bodies, from air they have their breath, from water they have their blood and from earth their bodies. (*CC* 49, 29)

Indeed, in a sense human beings can be said even to *contain* the world; for 'God imprinted every creature in humankind itself according to its measure' (*DW* 1, 2).

Elsewhere Hildegard not only sees a parallel between the 'humours of the body' and the winds which sweep the earth's surface, but she even suggests that the latter act directly upon the former: 'Then I noticed how the humours in the human organism are distributed and altered by various qualities of the wind and air, as soon as such qualities come into conflict with one another, because the humours themselves take on such qualities' (*DW* 3, 1).

For Hildegard, humanity, despite its special place in creation, is not distinct from the rest of creation. We are composed of the same elements, and our nature is constructed along the same principles, as the world in which we live. And, although the creatures have been made in order to serve our needs (*DW* 2, 2), we too are answerable to them:

> God has directed for humanity's benefit all of creation, which God has formed both on the heights and in the depths. If we abuse our position and commit evil deeds, God's judgement will permit other creatures to punish us. And just as creatures have to serve our bodily needs, it is also understood that they are intended for the welfare of our souls. (*DW* 3, 2)

Elsewhere she tells us how the elements will 'hold their right course' if our deeds are just, but will inflict suffering upon us if we 'perform evil deeds' (*DW* 4, 104). Hildegard's view of humanity then is one which suggests that we express our true nature when we are in harmony with creation, and she suggests that being sinful means that we are not in harmony with the world around us (*SC* III 5, 17).

As befits a world-scheme in which humankind has such a central place, Hildegard has a very 'high' view of human nature in that she believes that redeemed humanity is to take the place of the fallen angels before the throne of God (*DW* 1, 10). This positive view of humanity is balanced however by a keen sense of our sinfulness and our need for redemption through the saving action of Christ, to which theme the whole of the second part of *Scivias* is devoted. But what is characteristic above all of Hildegard's understanding of humanity is the belief that we and the creation are intrinsically *good*. The measure of our sinfulness is the measure of the distortion of that essential goodness within us. And we are good, according to Hildegard, because life itself is divinely given and is good. There is nothing of an unwholesome depreciation of ourselves or creation here, although Hildegard remains fully and realistically aware of our many failings which constantly serve to distort that image of goodness within us.

HILDEGARD'S IMAGERY

The whole of Hildegard's work is inspired by the spirit of balance and moderation.[23] Within the cosmic order of things, humankind (we who contain within ourselves the elements both of heaven and earth) represent a central mediating point located between the divine and the earthly. We are called ourselves to live in harmony 'with the elements'; to maintain a proper balance in all things so that the humours and the system of dryness and moisture within the body will be kept in ordered harmony. And the chief way in which this concern with *order* and *harmony* is expressed is by Hildegard's understanding of *health.* It is this motif which runs throughout the whole of her work, both when she is talking of the essential truths of the Christian revelation and of our moral life, as well as when she reflects on our physical state in her medical works. And the central, unifying image which she uses here in order to connect the different levels of her reflection is that of 'greenness' (Latin: *viriditas*).

At one level, the origin of this image must lie in the subtle, ever-changing and deeply affecting green of the hills that surround the Disibodenberg and Rupertsberg areas of the German Rhineland, where Hildegard lived and worked. And, in the first instance, greenness is the living life of the fruitful earth (e.g. 'The rivers give rise to smaller streams that sustain the earth by their greening power' (*DW* 4, 59)). The burgeoning life of the earth is founded upon moisture (rainfall) and upon the dynamic life-force which is ultimately the living energy of God and which, for Hildegard, generally takes the form of reproductive power. Although it sometimes has this sense in us too, the 'greenness' of humanity lies principally in our rational soul, which 'is the green life-force of the flesh' (*DW* 4, 21).

But Hildegard uses this image of the 'green' life-force of the world in order also to represent the spiritual life of grace and virtue, and Peter Dronke is quite right when he says that Hildegard's greenness 'is the earthly expression of the celestial sunlight; greenness is the condition in which earthly beings experience a fulfilment which is both physical and divine; greenness is the blithe overcoming of the dualism between earthly and heavenly'.[24] *Viriditas* in the natural order is linked with the moisture which is essential to life, and so, in the spiritual realm, moisture (rainfall, dewfall) is specifically linked with the Holy Spirit, the giver of Life: 'Through the Word, the sweet moisture of holiness fell from God and in the Holy Spirit' (*SC* II 1, 8). In another passage, the Holy Spirit itself is 'green': 'She [blessedness] is also surrounded with many gifts which are green with the greenness of the Holy Spirit' (*SC* III 6, 33), for it is the Holy Spirit 'which poured out this green freshness of life into the hearts of men and women so that they might bear good fruit' (*DW* 10, 2). Here Hildegard is adapting the green fruitfulness of the earth in order to express the virtues and good deeds of spiritual souls who are 'fecund' (*DW* 1, 16):

> If meanwhile, we give up the green vitality of these virtues and surrender to the drought of our indolence, so that we do not have the sap of life and the greening power of good deeds, then the power of our very soul will begin to fade and dry up . . . But if we follow the right road, all our actions will give rise to good fruit. (*DW* 2, 18)

There are other occasions too in which Hildegard uses the image of green-life to refer to different aspects of the divine order. Thus she says of the Church that it spreads 'like bursting buds and blessed greenness' (*SC* II 5, 26); the 'moist greenness' of a stone 'signifies God, who never becomes dry nor is limited in virtue' (*SC* II 2, 5); the 'greenness of life-giving breath' is 'brought forth from the mouth' of a priest who officiates at the Eucharist (*SC* II 6, 11); from 'tears and sighs the greening life-force of repentance arises' (*DW* 4, 32); in number nineteen of her *Songs*, the Virgin Mary is the 'greenest branch' and, in the *Book of Divine Works*, Jesus himself is 'the green wood because he caused all the greening power of the virtues' (*DW* 10, 19).

Behind Hildegard's image of 'greenness' (and indeed the rest of her colour imagery) is the central concept of light.[25] After all, the source of her visions is precisely the 'living light' together with the 'reflection of the living light',[26] and her writings abound in imagery which conveys this sense of radiance. Above all, the universe itself becomes a mirror which captures and throws back the divine light in a symphony of brilliance and grandeur. At the top of the hierarchy of creation are the angels, which are like 'the brilliance of many reflections in a mirror' (*DW* 1, 6). Men and women possess the power of reason, which is the noblest element in the soul and which Hildegard describes in terms of light so that 'we are flooded with light itself in the same way as the light of day illumines the world' (*DW* 4, 105). Similarly, Hildegard speaks of the 'dazzlingly fair wings of reason' on which we can 'soar upward in true faith and hope to God' (*DW* 7, 5). And finally, in one of Hildegard's most powerful images of all, the whole of creation is radiant with the divine light: 'all living creatures are, so to speak, sparks from the radiation of God's brilliance, and these sparks emerge from God like the rays of the sun' (*DW* 4, 11).

Hildegard the Woman

What kind of person was this extraordinary, enigmatic woman who made such an impact on her own times, only to disappear from view for nearly eight hundred years before being 'rediscovered' in our own century? By the end of her life Hildegard's fame had spread half way across Europe. People of all ranks visited her convent on the Rupertsberg to seek her advice in both spiritual and practical matters. Her fame as a counsellor equalled her reputation for healing and exorcism and her prophetic gifts led to comparisons with the Old Testament figures of Miriam, Deborah and Judith, whom she was said to excel. Hildegard inspired admiration and devotion from many of those around her, but like all powerful and forceful personalities, she also had her share of detractors.

Although Hildegard's writings sometimes appear contradictory and unsystematic, an examination of her works does give us some clues as to the kind of person we are dealing with. The picture of a highly intelligent, sensitive, forceful, artistic and well-integrated woman emerges. Hildegard is no pious innocent, despite her oblation (her dedication to monastic life as a child) and her relatively restricted experience of the world from within a Benedictine cloister. She can write with a detached enthusiasm about matters such as the pleasures of sexual intercourse, while at the same time developing a rich theology of the celibate life, which was celebrated with great splendour in her convent on the Rupertsberg. If Hildegard was your friend, she would stand by you, although never being afraid to correct where she thought necessary, but she was not a woman one would want as an enemy. Scathing and relentless in her criticism of those she thought were despoiling the Church of God, and determined in getting her own way, Hildegard was undoubtedly a force to be reckoned with. While we may not agree with all that Hildegard says and does – indeed much of her thinking and her behaviour bears a medieval stamp which can seem alien to our own concerns – one cannot help but respect her. There is a zest for life, a respect for individuals and for the created world, an irrepressible energy, an imaginative power and a yearning for the good and the beautiful which attract and fascinate those who come into contact with this remarkable woman. As a leading twentieth-century poet Stephan George, himself a native of Bingen, put it, 'Here is someone with whom one could have talked!'

HILDEGARD'S PERSONALITY

One way of learning more about Hildegard's personality is by examining some of her relationships as revealed in her letters. One of the most important people in Hildegard's life was undoubtedly Richardis of Stade, the nun who had been her confidante during their years at Disibodenberg. From the correspondence concerning Richardis's removal to a convent in the north of Germany, and her subsequent tragic death, we obtain a picture of an intimate, but perhaps overly dependent relationship, which Hildegard was loath to relinquish. From letters to Hazzecha of Krauftal, the abbess of a community in the diocese of Strasburg, we learn something of Hildegard's wisdom, compassion and common sense. Her key word in giving pastoral advice is 'discretion', and she displays a keen and sympathetic understanding of human frailty. A third significant relationship, of a different tenor altogether, was with the German emperor, Frederick Barbarossa, one of the most powerful men of his age. Thanks perhaps to her own noble background and to the aristocratic circles in which she moved, Hildegard felt herself competent to approach this maverick international statesman. They met personally on at least one occasion, and conducted a correspondence over many years.

HILDEGARD AND RICHARDIS OF STADE

An illustration from the Lucca manuscript of *The Book of Divine Works* shows Hildegard receiving her visions in a stream of heavenly light and writing them onto a tablet. Behind her stands a nun, presumed to be Richardis, and on the other side of a grille Volmar takes down and edits Hildegard's words. Richardis is represented as a collaborator, along with Volmar, in Hildegard's mission to 'write and tell' what she has seen and heard in her visions. But it is only when shortly after the move to the Rupertsberg Richardis threatens to leave Hildegard, that we learn just how much she meant to the abbess. Both Richardis and her niece Adelheid (the daughter of Liutgart, Richardis's younger sister) who was also a nun in Hildegard's convent, were elected abbesses of more prestigious foundations. Richardis was destined for the Benedictine abbey of Bassum in the diocese of Bremen, where her brother Hartwig was archbishop, and Adelheid for Gandersheim (and later Quedlinburg), despite the fact that she can have been little more than a child at the time of the appointment. The von Stades were numerous and well-placed, one of the leading families of their time. Liutgart had married well three times, her second husband being the King of Denmark. It is possible that the abbeys which elected the two women hoped to attract the family's support and endowments. It is also possible that the women themselves, with the help of their relatives, wished to obtain positions more in keeping with their status. While Hildegard was alive, no one else could play anything other than second fiddle on the Rupertsberg.

Whatever the circumstances, Hildegard was devastated at the prospect of losing Richardis. She was not, she argued, against Richardis's election in principle, if this were the will of God, but for the sake of her soul felt obliged to oppose a move undertaken solely on worldly grounds. Richardis herself seems to have been in favour of the move and Hildegard felt betrayed, coming as the move did amidst the hardships and criticisms which accompanied their first years on the Rupertsberg, a time when Hildegard most needed her friend's support. Hildegard appealed to Richardis's mother, the Marchioness of Stade, to the Archbishop of Mainz and even to Pope Eugenius III in an effort to block the appointment. Having failed in this, Hildegard directed her efforts towards

Richardis's brother, Hartwig, entreating him to persuade Richardis to return to Rupertsberg.

Hildegard's efforts were almost repaid, but Richardis died before she could make the journey. In the letter bearing the sad news, Hartwig assured Hildegard that Richardis had longed to return, and took the blame for her removal upon himself. In her answer Hildegard is able to express the love she felt for Richardis, and to forgive all those she had thought were scheming against her, but at the same time justifies her own position:

> Full divine love was in my soul towards her, for in the mightiest vision the living light taught me to love her. Listen: God kept her so jealously that worldly delight could not embrace her: she fought against it, even though she rose like a flower in the beauty and glory and symphony of this world . . .
>
> So my soul has great confidence in her, though the world loved her beautiful looks and her prudence, while she lived in the body. But God loved her more. Thus God did not wish to give her to a rival lover, that is, to the world . . . So I also expel from my heart that pain you caused me regarding this my daughter.[27]

Close monastic friendships were not frowned upon in the twelfth century as they came to be later. Both Bernard of Clairvaux and Aelred of Rievaulx, among others, had written treatises on the importance of friendship in community life.[28] There is, however, a possessiveness in Hildegard's attitude to Richardis which enables us to sympathize with the younger woman's desire for more autonomy, while feeling torn by her loyalty to her friend and mentor. This all too human relationship reveals Hildegard to be a woman of strong emotions, fierce in her attachments, but able to give in gracefully when all seems lost. The hurts inflicted by this experience, however, were not forgotten, and Hildegard returned to the incident at the end of her life when helping with the compilation of her *Vita*.

HILDEGARD AND ABBESS HAZZECHA OF KRAUFTAL

In her relationship with Hazzecha, abbess of Krauftal, Hildegard reveals a very different aspect of her character. Hildegard had visited the abbey in 1160 and found the community in disorder, the abbess unable to cope with her responsibilities. Hildegard's presence and words of advice seem to have struck the abbess forcefully, and Hazzecha continued to write to Hildegard after her return. She looked up to the seer and appeared to be dependent on her support in a way which Hildegard considered excessive, having perhaps learnt the lesson of so great a dependence in her own life. Hazzecha had conceived the idea of leaving her post for the life of a hermit, and sought Hildegard's approval. Recognizing that the abbess was prompted by a desire to escape her responsibilities rather than a genuine calling to the eremitical life, Hildegard counselled perseverance. If she failed as abbess, she would surely fail as an anchoress as well, leaving her worse off than before. In the letter to Hazzecha printed in this anthology, we can see that she has returned to her scheme. Hazzecha plans either to go on a pilgrimage to Rome, or to establish a hermitage with some chosen companions. Hildegard once more urges her to act with discretion, and not to ignore the advice of others out of pride or self-will. She tells Hazzecha frankly that her plans will do her no good, and promises to pray so that she may have the strength to persevere in her duties as abbess.

Here we have the mature Hildegard speaking with assurance, clarity and sympathetic good sense. She knows that what appears as piety can be a trap or an escape from reality, and that the hardest course, but also the truest, is to shoulder gracefully the burdens life gives us.[29]

HILDEGARD AND FREDERICK BARBAROSSA

Hildegard wrote letters of 'correction and advice' to numerous leading men and women of her day, including the German king, Conrad III, and his famous son, Emperor Frederick I (1152–90). We have the texts of three letters from Hildegard to Frederick and one reply, referring to a meeting they had at Ingelheim. The first letter from Hildegard was to congratulate Frederick on his election in 1152. She presented a most exalted view of leadership and of courtly values and invoked God's blessing upon him. In 1159 Alexander III was elected pope, but a minority of cardinals nominated an alternative candidate, Victor IV. Alexander III laid down a challenge to Frederick by claiming that the German crown was a 'benefice' bestowed by the pope. The theological argument for this was that the pope, as representative of Christ, was sovereign over all earthly rulers. Frederick, not surprisingly, supported the antipope, and was excommunicated by Alexander.

Hildegard sought a charter of protection from Frederick, which confirmed the Rupertsberg convent's possessions and rights as set out in the 1158 documents. Presumably the abbey's independence was still threatened by some of Hildegard's opponents. In a second letter, dated 18 April 1163, Hildegard thanks the Emperor for this charter but, addressing Frederick as 'Servant of God', reminds him that his worldly powers should serve a higher purpose than his own ambition. Only when he seeks God's Kingdom will Frederick, like King David in the Bible, be delivered from the hands of his enemies. On a more personal note, Hildegard undertakes to pray for the son and heir for which Frederick and his second wife, Beatrice, so long. Her prayers were answered for in July 1164 they had a boy, Frederick, followed in November 1165 by a second son, Henry.

The third of Hildegard's letters to Barbarossa is short and curt. In 1164 Victor IV died and Frederick elected a second antipope, Paschalis III. Hildegard accused Frederick of behaving childishly, like one who is insane, and warned him that the grace of God in his life was in danger of being extinguished. The fourth and final letter is even more terse, a series of biblical quotations warning of divine retribution for the wicked, sent after the election of a third antipope, Callistus III, in 1168.

From this correspondence, spanning two decades, we can glimpse something of Hildegard's sense of responsibility in her role as a prophet, exhorting, cajoling and, when necessary, condemning. It was not Frederick's expansionist ambitions so much as his opposition to the papacy which angered Hildegard, but she was tenacious in her determination to get the emperor to amend his ways. Her influence may not have been as great as she could have wished, but Hildegard continued to regard the affairs of state as part of her legitimate concerns.

That friendly relations were maintained between Frederick's family and the Rupertsberg cloister is attested by an entry in the abbey's record of the deceased of Empress Beatrice's death in 1184.

LIFE ON THE RUPERTSBERG

Life in the Rupertsberg convent contrasted starkly with Hildegard's early years as a hermit. Although they continued to follow the Benedictine Rule, the Rupertsberg nuns developed their own unusual and elaborate forms of dress and of worship. One of the rumours concerning the community, which had reached Guibert at Gembloux, was that Hildegard and her nuns wore tiaras or crowns. Was this, he wanted to know, due to divine revelation or merely indulging a taste for finery? (a weakness thought to be particularly feminine). In a long letter in which she attempts to answer his many questions, Hildegard reveals the extent to which daily life in her convent had become resonant with symbolic and visionary significance:

> As for tiaras: I saw that all the ranks of the Church have bright emblems in accord with the heavenly brightness, yet virginity has no bright emblem – nothing but a black veil and an image of the cross. So I saw that this would be the emblem of virginity: that a virgin's head would be covered with a white veil, because of the radiant-white robe that human beings had in paradise, and lost. On her head would be a circlet with three colours conjoined into one – an image of the Trinity – and four roundels attached: the one on the forehead showing the lamb of God, that on the right a cherub, that on the left an angel, and on the back a human being – all these inclining towards the Trinity. This emblem, granted to me, will proclaim blessings to God, because he had clothed the first man in radiant brightness.[30]

It is possible, as A. M. Allchin suggests, that these tiaras or crowns were like the simple cloth circlets worn by Bridgettine nuns today,[31] but, whatever their appearance, their purpose was clear. The consecrated virgin could reclaim a paradisal state, uncontaminated by the fall, and while still on earth should celebrate the Kingdom of heaven in all its beauty and extravagance.

The costumes devised by Hildegard for her nuns are clearly inspired by her visions. In her *Book of Life's Merits* (6.43 and 44), Hildegard sees the blessed virgins in paradise 'clothed in gowns of purest gold and decked with precious jewels', and 'on their heads they wore golden crowns studded with gems and interwoven with roses and lilies'. Only those privileged to wear the crowns could hear the wonderful and harmonious music of heaven and take pleasure in it.

Rumours of unusual practices on the Rupertsberg had also reached Tengswindis (Tengswich), the leader of a foundation of canonesses at St Marien near Andernach. In a polite but guardedly critical letter Tengswindis asked Hildegard about the costumes worn by her nuns, and sought clarification concerning her community's practice of admitting only women of noble birth. This was perhaps a somewhat disingenuous question as the canoness orders were normally open only to aristocratic women. The Benedictine houses, on the other hand, were divided as to whether their members should be recruited from all classes, as the Rule of St Benedict recommended, or restricted to noble men and women only. The Rupertsberg, it would appear, followed the latter line, although the earliest monastery book of remembrance records the presence of 'nuns', who were nobly born, of 'sisters', who were presumably from more humble backgrounds, and of 'lay women', all of whom would have formed part of the community.[32] Hildegard, however, defends a degree of exclusivity, claiming authority for her words from 'the living fountain'. Her thinking follows the social mores of her day, rather than the more revolutionary gospel (or Benedictine) notions of equality. What farmer, she asks, would put oxen, asses, sheep and goats in a single field? They would all scatter, and so would different classes of human beings. They would tear one another apart in hate, those of higher rank setting themselves above the lower, and those of lower rank seeking to rise above the higher. For Hildegard, human hierarchies are ordained by God, people are ranked like the angels; equally loved, but not to be confused.

In practical terms Hildegard may have had a point. No doubt it was easier to rule over a community in which each knew their place, and in which the noble women in her charge had no excuse to lord it over others. It is only in the last few decades that many of the present religious orders have done away with the divisions between choir and lay brothers or sisters, or have admitted African, Asian or South American religious on an equal footing. Hildegard may not have been right in Christian terms, but she was not the first or the last person to confuse the divine order with human social constructs.

The importance of music in the Rupertsberg convent is also well attested. Hildegard had begun composing her own liturgical songs and music, based on monastic plainsong, during her years on the Disibodenberg, and under the inspiration of her visions she continued with this work at Rupertsberg. Some of Hildegard's music has recently been recorded and performed, and, as with so much of her work, appears startlingly modern and original. For Hildegard, music was more than a way of praising God, it was a way of sharing in the life of heaven itself. Through music, human beings are reminded of the harmonies of the heavenly spheres, indeed, the soul itself is symphonic.

When, in the last years of her life, Hildegard's community was placed under an interdict by the prelates of Mainz for allowing the burial in consecrated ground of a man who had been excommunicated, the greatest hardship they endured was the absence of music. Hildegard never tired in her efforts to have the interdict lifted and it is in her letters to these priests that we learn of the central place music played in the life of the Rupertsberg community.[33] In obeying the Mainz prelates, Hildegard felt that she was disobeying God, and she struggled to reconcile her duty to her inner voice and to the Church.

When, after her death, a commission was set up to seek witnesses for Hildegard's canonization, three of her sisters swore that they had seen Hildegard illuminated by the Holy Spirit as she walked through the cloisters chanting one of her favourite compositions.[34] It was above all through music that the unity of the human and divine could be realized and the Rupertsberg convent appears to have been a place where the harmonies of heaven were celebrated on earth in all their fullness.

Hildegard held extremely exalted views of the monastic vocation, placing monks and nuns above priests and bishops, who were in turn ranked higher than ordinary lay people. While it was possible to aspire to a higher order, to descend from a higher to a lower state was not to be countenanced (SC II 5, 35). The monastic vocation should not, according to Hildegard, be adopted hastily or for impure motives, as once an individual had made their vows there was no turning back. Hildegard even suggested that those wishing to leave the monastic life should be confined and kept on bread and water. She therefore warns against sending children to a monastery against their will and condemns the use of religious life as an escape from poverty, bodily weakness or personal troubles.

The atmosphere in the Rupertsberg convent can only be surmised. From her extensive writings on human physiology, on medicine, psychology, and what we would today term psychotherapy, it is clear that not only the spiritual aspect of the nuns' lives received attention. What does seem clear is that life on the Rupertsberg had an intensely mystical flavour. This can be glimpsed not only from their clothes and music, but also from a puzzle that has intrigued students of Hildegard for many years. Among Hildegard's works is an 'unknown language' (Lingua ignota) with its own 'unknown alphabet'. It survives in a glossary of some nine hundred words which refer to items of everyday use, such as the clothes worn by the nuns and the herbs in the garden, as well as to all manner of natural and heavenly beings. A few words of her secret language find their way into some of Hildegard's songs, particularly the antiphon 'O orzchis Ecclesia'.

This language was evidently important to Hildegard and, like her music and the designs for the nuns' liturgical habits, was an attempt to imitate what she saw and heard in her visions. Hildegard wrote to Pope Anastasius IV in 1153/4 that she had been inspired by God to 'form unknown letters, and utter an unknown language, and to resound with melody in many tones'. Her Vita also records that she 'composed chant of surpassingly sweet melody with amazing harmony, and invented letters never seen before, with a language hitherto unheard'.[35] The purpose of the language and its twenty-three letter alphabet is not entirely clear. It has been dismissed as a mental exercise, and hailed as an early insight into the genetic code! Barbara Newman is probably on the right track, however, when she links it to Hildegard's music and to the mystical life of the community.[36] We should not be surprised that an imagination as creative and an intelligence as keen as Hildegard's delighted in such invention, a delight shared, incidentally, by her compatriot and admirer, Stephan George, some eight hundred years later.

AN EFFEMINATE AGE

Reading Hildegard we sense that we are in the presence of a woman who was at peace with herself and who had made sense of her place in the great scheme of creation. Hildegard sought constantly to integrate all aspects of life. The supernatural realm, the natural world around her, human beings with their corporeal existence; all were intimately related and subject to the same laws. There is no aspect of life which did not interest Hildegard and which did not come under the scrutiny of her inner light. There are however contradictions within Hildegard's writings and she adopts a somewhat different style when speaking as a theologian and when speaking as a medical practitioner or natural scientist. It is not surprising, given the scope of her works and the attitudes of the time, that she did not always achieve the synthesis which she had intended.

Hildegard held certain traditional views of gender relations. Women were seen as frailer than men, more diffuse in their energies, more passive and (unusually for the period) were thought to be weaker in their sexual appetites. Both male and female visionary writers of the twelfth century referred to themselves as 'weak women', a term which had become a topos of humility, but which, when directed at women by others, was used to disparage their works and to undermine their authority. Her behaviour, however, departed from conventional female stereotypes and Hildegard succeeded in turning prevailing categories on their head. She referred to hers as an 'effeminate age'. Because men had become 'womanish', God would make women virile. Traditional sex roles were reversed; female authority was presented as a restitution of the natural order, not as a threat or challenge to it. In a letter to a negligent bishop Hildegard described a vision of Pure Knowledge as a female figure dressed in a bishop's pallium. This female role model might well have been intended as a representation of Hildegard herself in her role as prophet.[37] In her visions Hildegard saw the Church, the Synagogue and the virtues as female figures, but certainly not as weak ones. Her 'living light' was none other than Wisdom, the female aspect of the Godhead.

It is as though conventional sexual stereotypes never tell the whole story, and Hildegard is continually modifying and subverting them. She has strong intuitions about the interdependence and complementarity of all aspects of the world, including men and women. In an exegesis of the scriptural passage on the capable woman (Proverbs 31.10–11), Hildegard describes strength and weakness as common to both men and women. Woman's strength is seen as more supple and flexible than man's (*LM* 28, 36). In another passage (*DW* 5, 43) Hildegard explains how a man has greater strength and a woman softer energy. The incarnation itself is seen as a coming together of the strength of God and the frailty of humanity: 'And the divinity is strong while the flesh of the Son of God is frail, that flesh by which the world is restored to its original life' (*LM* 4, 36).[38]

Hildegard's belief in the complementarity of the sexes also emerges in her interpretation of the passage from 1 Cor. 11.9, 'For the man was not created for the woman but the woman for the man', which Hildegard modifies according to her own philosophy:

> Thus it is written: *Woman is created for the man* and the man is made for woman, since as she is made from man and man from her, neither is separated from the other in the unity of producing offspring, because they produce one thing in a single work just as air and wind are each involved in the work of the other.[39]

Her notion of the complementarity of the sexes led Hildegard to reject homosexuality, which was seen as not only against biblical injunction, but also in contravention of the natural order. Of male homosexuality Hildegard wrote: 'But these perverse adulterers, when they change their manly strength into the contrary weakness, casting aside the true nature of male and female, most foully imitate Satan in their perversity who wished to destroy and divide Him who is indivisible, in his pride' (SC II 6, 78).[40] Similarly with lesbian sexuality, it was the assumption of another's role and the consequent disruption of God's intention to unite man and woman which worried Hildegard.

THE GARDEN OF EDEN

One would not expect a cloistered nun to have a wide experience of human sexuality, but through her contact with ordinary lay people, with whom she must have talked intimately and at great length, Hildegard displayed a remarkable sympathy for and knowledge of this aspect of human behaviour. She was also, as A. M. Allchin has remarked, virtually alone among the writers of the Middle Ages in treating medical and psychological problems from a woman's point of view.[41] In a passage from her scientific and medical book, *Causes and Cures*, for example, Hildegard writes the following about the erotic delight of sexual intercourse:

> When a woman is making love with a man, a sense of heat in her brain, which brings with it sensual delight, communicates the taste of that delight during the act and summons forth the emission of the man's seed. And when the seed has fallen into its place, that vehement heat descending from her brain draws the seed to itself and holds it, and soon the woman's sexual organs contract, and all the parts that are ready to open up during the time of menstruation now close, in the same way as a strong man can hold something enclosed in his fist.[42]

When writing as a theologian, rather than as a physiologist, Hildegard follows more traditional Church teachings on the impurity of sex. Although never quite adopting the dualist position of the Cathars, who saw all bodily functions as inimical to the spiritual life, Hildegard nevertheless regards sexuality as a result of humanity's fallen state.

It is quite clear from Hildegard's descriptions of paradise that human sexuality as we know it had no place. The love of Adam and Eve for one another before the fall is contrasted with the lust of man in his fallen state:

> When man transgressed God's command, he was changed both in body and mind. For the purity of his blood was turned into another mode, so that, instead of purity, he now ejects the spume of semen. If man had remained in paradise, he would have stayed in an immutable and perfect state. But all these things, after his transgression, were turned into another and bitter mode. For man's blood, burning in the ardour and heat of lust, ejects a spume from itself that we call semen, as a pot placed on the fire brings up foam from the water because of the flame's heat.[43]

Hildegard likewise believed that in paradise children were conceived without intercourse and delivered, as Mary gave birth to Jesus, through the woman's side. It is in the renunciation of sexual relations that the consecrated virgin can recapture the lost delights of paradise, and enjoy the heavenly music which Adam lost through his fall into concupiscence.

HILDEGARD THE HEALER

Hildegard was widely sought by all manner of people as a healer, exorcist and psychotherapist. Women in general, and nuns in particular, were regarded as knowledgeable in medical matters, and monastic gardens grew a range of therapeutic plants. Some women, such as Trotula, an eleventh-century woman who taught at Europe's most distinguished medical school at Salerno in Italy and who wrote a book on women's diseases, were famed as surgeons and doctors. Other women practised midwifery or herbalism locally, and passed on their knowledge to their daughters. It was not until the thirteenth century that concerted efforts to exclude women from the practice of medicine gathered pace. Hildegard had not made a formal study of medicine and presumably garnered much of her knowledge of disease and of healing plants and other treatments from the traditional folk wisdom of her locality. With her acute sense of observation, and guided by her own perceptive imagination and intuitions, Hildegard built up a vast store of medical knowledge.

It is for her dietary and medical writings that Hildegard has attracted most popular attention in her native Germany, thanks mainly to the dedicated work of a small number of practitioners of Hildegard medicine who have sought to test and to put into practice the cures suggested by the seer. Most of Hildegard's medical writings are to be found in two books, *Physica* and *Causae et curae*. Hildegard does not present these scientific and medical writings in the form of visions, nor are they claimed as a direct transmission from the living light (unless a general introduction, similar to that in her visionary works, has been lost).

Much of Hildegard's advice seems eminently sensible and was no doubt put into practice in her convent and elsewhere. She recommends a balanced diet, sufficient rest, the alleviation of stress and a wholesome moral life. Some of her more exotic treatments must have been more difficult to put into effect. Ostriches, whales, vultures, lions and leopards are all listed with their healing properties. The use of various rare precious stones and metals recommended by Hildegard also sounds unlikely in practice.

All diseases and cures were linked to Hildegard's understanding of the four qualities of heat, dryness, moistness, and cold; the corresponding elements – fire, air, water and earth; and the humours and personality types to which the elements give rise. The aim of medical practice was to achieve a balance in these elements, which had been upset through an inherited disposition or because of sickness. Astrological influences and the moon were also thought to affect personality and physique, but whatever the predetermined disposition of a person, they could allow God to use them for the furtherance of his work.

We have little information concerning actual occurrences of physical healing but there is an account in Hildegard's *Life* of a lengthy exorcism performed on a woman called Sigewize.[44] In

1167, during a period of sickness, Hildegard was told that a young noblewoman from the lower Rhine was being tormented by a demon. According to Hildegard, demons could not enter or possess people but they could envelop and obsess them. The demon troubling Sigewize had declared that only Hildegard (referred to irreverently as 'Scrumpilgardis' or 'Wrinklegard') could help. Because of her infirmity Hildegard did not want to treat Sigewize in person, but she wrote a therapeutic drama for her which was to be performed with great ceremony and seriousness (reminiscent of a shamanic journey in which the sick person takes part with their imagination). A temporary improvement followed its performance, but in the end Hildegard acceded to Sigewize's pleadings to be treated in person and took her into the Rupertsberg convent. Hildegard and the nuns were terrified at the prospect and endured with difficulty the young woman's wild and frightening behaviour. Their method of treatment was communal prayer and ascetic practices. In this secure and supportive environment the demon was allowed full expression and gradually Sigewize's mental instability subsided and her health returned. Hildegard claimed no miraculous powers, but displayed sound psychotherapeutic judgement, compassion and common sense, a combination which achieved the desired result.

Hildegard's extensive works are so varied in their style and content that some commentators have doubted that they could all come from the same pen. Hildegard was an extraordinarily gifted individual with talents and interests in many different directions. We can be thankful that she overcame the limitations of her gender, her infirmities and her background and that she was able to exercise her abilities and to leave a record of her achievements for posterity. Hildegard is not an easy figure to assimilate. The volume of her writing, the obscurity of much of her thinking, the idiosyncrasies of her Latin, all conspire to reduce her accessibility to the modern reader. Much remains to be done in the field of Hildegard scholarship, in particular in the critical editing of her works. There is no doubt, however, that engaging with Hildegard is a rewarding experience. She has the ability to speak to us powerfully across the centuries, illuminating other minds with her living light.

Hildegard Today

The rapid growth of interest in Hildegard over the last two decades, both among the circles of the learned and in the populace at large, is a powerful testimony to her relevance for us today. And the reasons for this are perhaps not difficult to fathom. We find in Hildegard a brilliantly original and remarkably *balanced* view of the universe. And while humanity stands at the centre of creation according to her system, we are meshed into it at all points. Our own nature, the rhythms of our minds and bodies, are an echo of the greater rhythms of the natural world; we do not exist in isolation, then, but are parts of an encompassing whole. And so it would not be appropriate to think of humankind as standing imperially outside the world; rather we are answerable to it in that the source of our life is the same as the life-source of all things: namely, the divine ebullience, the overflow of divine light and love. And just like the creation itself, we capture and reflect something of that primal light. Hence we are fundamentally good, and the state of sin in which we find ourselves is to be understood as a distortion of that goodness, which serves to 'cloud' that original light.

Secondly, Hildegard was an immensely gifted woman whose capacity to clothe ancient, resonant truths in language which was itself transfigured and transfiguring was truly remarkable. We have seen the extraordinary suppleness and power of her imagery of greenness, living and moist, which seems to capture the very essence of a natural and a divine fecundity. Her images of 'light' and 'reflection' ('clarity', 'radiance', 'brilliance', 'luminosity', 'fire' and 'flame'); her world of flashing gems (sapphires, onyx, rubies, diamond); her world of shining colours all conspire to convey to us a sense of the radiance of her own visions: of her own 'living light'. To spend time with Hildegard then purifies and uplifts the senses, so that we feel as we do when we walk out into the brilliant, blinding freshness of the first snow and are filled with wonder at the glory of God's creation and at the mystery of his incarnate Son.

Notes

1. *Historia Novorum*, p. 150. Quoted in Southern (1967), p. 129.
2. The major sources for Hildegard's life are the biography by Godfrey and Theodoric (which dates from the final quarter of the twelfth century and which includes much autobiographical material) and a fragmentary biography by Guibert of Gembloux. See bibliography for details. See Newman (1987), p. 5 for additional sources relevant to the reconstruction of Hildegard's life. There is an important summary of Hildegard's life by Adelgundis Führkötter in the Hildegard *Festschrift* ed. Brück (1979), pp. 31–55, and there are two fine full-scale biographies of Hildegard, by Eduard Gronau (1985) in German, and Sabina Flanagan (1989) in English.
3. Information concerning Disibodenberg is contained in the *Annales Sancti Disibodi*, Monumenta Germanica Historica SS. XVII, and in Brück (1979). There is also a booklet, *Der Disibodenberg*, tracing the history of the monastery, which contains a further bibliography (available from St Hildegardis Abbey, Eibingen).
4. According to her *Vita*, the vision which initiated the writing of *Scivias* came to her 'in her fortieth year'. Hildegard seems here to have reckoned her birth as in 1100.
5. Newman (1985), pp. 169–70.
6. A point made by Caroline Walker Bynum (1984), p. 185, who compares the writings of the beguine mystic, Mechthild of Magdeburg, with those of her younger monastic contemporaries, Gertrude the Great and Mechthild of Hackeborn.
7. Flanagan (1989), p. 6.
8. Petroff (1986), p. 6.
9. Dronke (1984), pp. 162–3.
10. Singer (1917, reprinted 1958). The migraine theory has been popularized by Clifford Rose and Gawel (1981), and Sacks (1986). The question is treated at length in Flanagan (1989), ch. 10.

11. The visionary experiences of these women are described in the introduction to *Beguine Spirituality*, ed. Bowie (1989).
12. Dronke (1984), p. 153–4.
13. Newman (1985), p. 171.
14. ibid.
15. This is well expressed in the prologue to the *Book of Divine Works*, where the 'voice from heaven' says: 'Commit to writing for the benefit of humankind and in enduring form what you see with your inner eyes and perceive with the inner ears of your soul so that, through these things, people may come to know their Creator and not recoil from worshipping him with the reverence due to him.'
16. Hildegard's work is not easily summarized, but one of the best attempts to do so is that by Heinrich Schipperges in Führkötter (1987).
17. It is interesting that Hildegard seems to be giving pride of place among the virtues here to poverty of spirit. In this she would seem to anticipate later developments in the Rhineland (Meister Eckhart and Johannes Tauler) in which this is emphatically the case.
18. It is this orientation also which distinguishes Hildegard from some of the later women visionary mystics. Unlike her great compatriots, Mechthild of Magdeburg and Gertrude the Great for instance, Hildegard is concerned primarily to instruct her audience in the mysteries of the Christian revelation, and not to express in a poetic voice the deepest stirrings of her spirit. It is this fact which led some to speak of Hildegard as a 'prophetess' in her own lifetime and to compare her with Deborah (e.g. *Vita*, II, Prologue and ch. 6). Cf. Margot Schmidt's excellent article on this theme, 'Hildegard von Bingen als Lehrerin des Glaubens', in Führkötter (1972), pp. 95–157.
19. Newman (1987), p. 64.
20. This is, of course, the doctrine of exemplarism, which is given an important impetus in the Middle Ages by Augustine.
21. Hildegard has much in common, therefore, with a later 'vitalism'. There are key differences, however, in that for Hildegard, the life of nature, while truly existing in itself, is transparent to its source, which is the divine life. Hildegard also has a strong sense of the *order* of things and of the necessarily harmonious proportions and relations of all that exists. In Nietzsche's terms, the Dionysian is well balanced by the Apollonian, therefore.
22. *Unde et homo opus Dei cum omni creatura est. Sed et homo operarius divinitatis esse dicitur* (*PL* 197, 116C).

23. It is worth recalling that a primary source for Hildegard's inspi-
    ration must have been the Benedictine Rule, by which she lived,
    and which is justly famed for its wise sense of moderation and the
    avoidance of extremes.
24. 'Tradition and Innovation in Medieval Western Colour-Imagery'
    in Dronke (1984), p. 84 (first published in *Eranos Jahrbuch* XLI
    (1972), pp. 51–106). See also 'Die Bedeutung der Farben im Werk
    Hildegards von Bingen' by Christel Maier in *Frühmittelalterliche
    Studien*, 6 (1972), especially pp. 280ff. and 285, in which Maier
    establishes the relation in Hildegard's work between the colours
    and the virtues.
25. It is important to see Hildegard within the tradition of those major
    theologians, such as Pseudo-Denys and Scotus Eriugena, who
    make extensive use of light imagery. Joseph Koch has written an
    interesting article on this theme, 'Über die Lichtsymbolik im
    Bereich der Philosophie', in *Kleine Schriften*, I, Rome (1973), pp.
    27–67 (first published in *Studium Generale* 13 (1960), pp. 653–70).
26. I am translating *umbra* here as 'reflection' rather than 'shadow',
    which appears to make more sense in the context of Hildegard's
    water imagery. *Umbra* is a word which suggests 'reflection', the
    communication of a quality from one subject to another, but also
    suggests 'shadow' or 'shade', which may signify the darkness
    which is absence of light, or indeed, the darkness which is excess
    of light. In Hildegard the secondary word *obumbratio* is also vitally
    important, and it has the added association of being the Vulgate
    translation for the 'overshadowing' of Mary by the Holy Spirit
    (Luke 1.35). There is an interesting article on the word *umbra* by
    Peter Dronke in his *The Medieval Poet and his World* (Rome 1984),
    'Theologia veluti quaedam poetria*: Quelques observations sur la
    fonction des images poétiques chez Jean Scot' (pp. 39–53; first
    published in *Jean Scot Erigène et l'histoire de la philosophie*, ed.
    R. Roques, Colloques Internationaux du CRNS No. 561, Paris
    (1977), pp. 243–52). Image and reflection, and the theme of the
    mirror, is the subject of Margot Schmidt's penetrating article in
    Führkötter (1972). Reflected radiance, as the communication of
    faith, grace, love and glory, is shown to be central to Hildegard's
    work.
27. Dronke (1984), p. 159.
28. See Bynum (1984), pp. 64–5.
29. For the texts of Hildegard's letters see *PL* 197; Dronke (1984),
    pp. 186–7 and Führkötter (1965), pp. 207ff.
30. Dronke (1984), p. 169.
31. Allchin (1989), p. 134. Hildegard's descriptions of the garments

worn by the blessed in heaven, and emulated by her own nuns, are strongly reminiscent of the prophet Ezekiel's account of Jerusalem, decked as God's bride (16, 8–14).

32. Führkötter (1965), p. 204. For the details of the correspondence between Hildegard and Tengswindis and for some discussion on it see Führkötter (1965), pp. 204–5, and Dronke (1984), pp. 165 –71.
33. Hildegard's correspondence with the Mainz prelates is discussed in Führkötter (1965), pp. 235–46, and Dronke (1984), pp. 196–9.
34. Newman (1988), p. 277.
35. Newman (1988), p. 316. See also Führkötter (1965), pp. 8–41, *PL* 197: 152d; *Vita*, *PL* 197: 101b.
36. Newman (1988), p. 18.
37. Newman (1985), p. 174.
38. Cited in Zum Brunn and Epiney-Burgard (1989), p. 14.
39. Cited in Bynum (1984), pp. 93–4.
40. Cited in Flanagan (1989), p. 69.
41. Allchin (1989), p. 137.
42. Cited in Dronke (1984), p. 175.
43. Cited in Dronke (1984), pp. 176–7.
44. An account of this exorcism is to be found in Dronke (1984), pp. 163–5.

A Short Chronology of Hildegard's Life

1098	Hildegard's birth at Bermersheim near Alzey in Rheinhessen. She is the tenth and last child of Hildebert of Bermersheim and his wife Mechthild.
1106	Hildegard enters an enclosure, with Jutta of Spanheim, which is attached to the recently founded Benedictine monastery of Disibodenberg. Jutta becomes her teacher.
1112–15	Hildegard takes her vows and receives the veil from Bishop Otto of Bamberg. The enclosure grows and becomes a convent.
1136	Death of Jutta of Spanheim. The nuns elect Hildegard as their leader.
1141	Hildegard begins to write *Scivias*. Her friend, the monk Volmar, and the nun Richardis of Stade act as her secretaries.
1146/47	Hildegard exchanges letters with Bernard of Clairvaux.
1147/48	Pope Eugenius III reads from *Scivias* at the Synod of Trier. He authorizes Hildegard to continue her work. Hildegard begins to correspond with many distinguished people. Hildegard is inspired by God to move from Disibodenberg to Rupertsberg, which she successfully initiates against the wishes of the monks.
1148	A letter from Master Odo of Paris reveals that Hildegard's songs are already well known.
1150	Hildegard moves to Rupertsberg with some eighteen or twenty nuns.

1151–58	Composition of the *Natural History* and of *Causes and Cures*.
1151	Finishes *Scivias*. Richardis accepts election as abbess of a convent at Bassum, near Bremen, against Hildegard's wishes.
1152	Frederick I (Barbarossa) is elected King. Hildegard writes him a letter in tribute. Richardis dies.
After 1154	Hildegard meets Frederick I at Ingelheim.
1155	Hildegard persuades the monks of Disibodenberg to relinquish the lands given as part of the nuns' dowry.
1158–61	Hildegard falls ill. She undertakes her first preaching tour, which takes her along the River Main as far as Bamberg.
1158–63	Composition of the *Book of Life's Merits*.
1159	Beginning of the eighteen-year long schism between the papacy and Frederick I. First antipope is Victor IV.
1160	Hildegard's second preaching tour. She preaches publicly in Trier, and then proceeds by way of Metz and Krauftal to Hördt.
1161–63	Hildegard's third preaching tour, following the Rhine northwards to Cologne, and then on to Werden.
1163	She begins to write the *Book of Divine Works*. She writes again to Frederick I, and appears to adopt a neutral position in the schism.
1164	Second antipope, Paschal III. Hildegard writes for a third time to Frederick, this time adopting a critical tone.
Around 1165	Hildegard founds the community at Eibingen, overlooking Rudesheim, on the east bank on the Rhine, which she visits twice a week. She writes to Henry II of England and to his wife, Queen Eleanor.

1167–70	Hildegard falls ill again.
1168	Third antipope, Callistus III. Hildegard writes to Frederick I, warning him of divine judgement.
1169	Hildegard heals the possessed woman, Sigewize, and receives her into her community at Rupertsberg.
1170	Composition of the *Life of St Disibod* at request of Abbot Helenger of Disibodenberg.
1170(71)	Hildegard's fourth preaching tour, which takes her south to Zwiefalten.
1173	Volmar, her secretary, dies.
1173/74	She completes the *Book of Divine Works*. A conflict arises regarding the appointment of Volmar's successor.
1174(75)	The monk Gottfried arrives from Disibodenberg. He begins to write the *Life of Hildegard* and completes Book One.
1175	Guibert of Gembloux begins a correspondence with Hildegard. She sends him her *Book of Life's Merits* and her *Songs*.
1176	Gottfried dies.
1177	Guibert of Gembloux becomes Hildegard's secretary.
1178	Interdict imposed on Rupertsberg by diocese of Mainz.
1179	Interdict lifted by Archbishop Christian of Mainz. Hildegard dies on 17 September.
1180–90	Theodoric of Echternach completes Books Two and Three of the *Life of Hildegard*.

PART 2

Selections

TRANSLATOR'S NOTE

No translator of Hildegard can be unmoved by the injunction she appends to the *Book of Divine Works*: 'Let no one . . . be so presumptuous as to add anything to the words of what is written here or take anything away, on pain of being erased from the Book of Life and from all the blessedness under the sun . . . Whoever presumes to do otherwise, sins against the Holy Spirit and will not be forgiven in this world or the next.'

Hildegard's claim to have set down words 'brought forth directly through the inspiration of the Holy Spirit' imposes a heavy task upon anyone attempting to transmute celestial Latin into mundane vernacular. By presenting a selection from her writings, divested of all that is repellent to modern sensibilities, we are, doubtless, already damned.

Hildegard never pretends to be a great Latin stylist, repeatedly emphasizing her own ignorance (*homo indocta sum*) and informing Guibert of Gembloux that she has not been 'taught in this vision to write as the philosophers write'. The stylistic shortcomings of her visionary works might be attributable to the pressure of divine inspiration; though no such excuse is available for her letters. Hildegard is capable of writing with a simplicity and grace that are truly moving. Yet the beauty of what she is describing is often marred by the ineptitude of her expression. At such times, it is difficult, at least for the jaundiced *littérateur*, to reconcile the rankness of the Latin with the divinity of its source. She heaps sentence upon sentence, loosely joined by conjunctions, with scant regard for the niceties of style or syntax, offending as much through pleonasmus as ellipsis. I have made no attempt to reproduce such vagaries in English. In the interest of intelligibility, long sentences have been divided up. In a few passages (most notably the opening of the letter to Bernard of Clairvaux) I have resorted to paraphrase.

It has not proved easy to adapt Hildegard to meet the editorial requirements of inclusive language. In translating *homo* and *homines*, I have adopted the practice of Barbara Newman, as outlined in her preface to *Sister of Wisdom* (1987). The plural presents few difficulties. I have rendered *homines* as 'people', 'humans' or 'mortals' except where it is clear from the context that the *homines* referred to are exclusively male. The singular is much more problematic. For Hildegard, *homo* is almost always an *inclusive* term, conveying the same range of meaning that has, traditionally, been provided in English by 'man'. It is a source of regret that there is no real English equivalent to the German, *Mensch*. The semantic field of 'Man' has contracted in recent years and terms like 'humankind' and 'humanity' have become current in its stead.

Previous translators of Hildegard (Ronald Miller in the *Letters*, Robert Cunningham in the *Book of Divine Works* and Bruce Hozeski in *Scivias*) have been rigorous, to the point of travesty, in their use of inclusive language, removing personal pronouns for God, translating *homo* as 'we' when the voice of the Living Light is speaking, and even, in Hozeski's case, rendering 'Son of God' as 'Word of God'.[1] Neither Hildegard nor feminism seems to be well served by such mendacities. Hildegard pays lip service to the prevailing medieval order, de-preciating her role as a 'poor little figure of a woman' even as she berates wayward kings and corrupt popes. Paradoxically, in order to see, in relief, the true originality of Hildegard's vision of the feminine in God, we need to preserve her differentiation of gender, resisting the temptation to rewrite a twelfth-century mystic as a twentieth-century feminist. Newman retains 'the singular collective *man* for a very frequent medieval usage in which *homo* simultaneously designates the human race and the unique individual Adam, in whom the whole race is seminally present.'[2] I have followed Newman's example.

The choice of Latin texts has been necessarily eclectic. Until the establishment of critical editions of all Hildegard's works, any transla-tion must be considered an interim measure. For the *Letters* and the *Book of Divine Works*, we are still largely reliant on J. P. Migne's edition of Hildegard (*PL*, 197, 1855), although Pitra supplies the text for my translation of the letter of Henry II of England and both Pitra and Dronke provide separate texts for the letter to Guibert of Gembloux.[3] Heinrich Schipperges' *Welt und Mensch: Das Buch 'De operatione Dei'*, is based on the unpublished Ghent manuscript and I have been able to supplement Migne's text from the list of variants appended to the German translation.[4] For the *Scivias*, we are fortunate in having the critical edition by Adelgundis Führkötter and Angela Carlevaris published in *Corpus Christianorum: Continuatio Mediaeualis*, Vols. 43 and 43A (Turnhout: Brepols, 1978).

I have, in all cases, translated directly from the Latin, subsequently revising my version in response to divergent readings noted by Oliver Davies in the German text.

Robert Carver
Worcester College, Oxford

1. Cunningham and Miller's translations appear in *Hildegard of Bingen's Book of Divine Works*, ed. Matthew Fox (Santa Fé: Bear & Company, 1987). Bruce Hozeski, tr., *Scivias by Hildegard of Bingen* (Santa Fé: Bear & Company, 1986).
2. Barbara Newman, *Sister of Wisdom: St Hildegard's Theology of the Feminine* (Aldershot: Scolar Press, 1987), p. xix.
3. J. B. Pitra, ed., *Analecta Sacra Spicilegio Solesmensi* Tom. VIII (Paris: Jouby & Roger, 1882), pp. 556 and 331ff. Peter Dronke, *Women Writers of the Middle Ages* (Cambridge: CUP, 1984), pp. 250ff. I have collated the two editions of the Guibert letter and moved rather freely between them.
4. Salzburg: Otto Müller Verlag (1965).

EDITORS' NOTE

The Extracts from the *Life of Saint Hildegard* by Godfrey and Theodoric, the passages from *Causes and Cures* and the following letters: Richardis von Stade, Abbess Hazzecha of Krauftal, Letter to an Abbot, Abbot Ludwig of St Eucharius, and the Mainz Prelates, are translated by Peter Dronke and are reprinted from *Women Writers of the Middle Ages*, Cambridge University Press, 1984. We would like to thank Professor Dronke and Cambridge University Press for their kind permission to reprint these extracts. The references following the passages from Hildegard's *Life* refer to the Berlin Manuscript, Staatsbibl. Lat. Qu. 674, fols. 1ra–24vb (see Dronke (1984), pp. 240–1).

The selections from *The Book of Life's Merits* were translated by Mark Atherton and Oliver Davies, using Pitra but also with reference to Schipperges' modern German translation. The *Songs* were translated by Oliver Davies from Barbara Newman's critical edition of the *Symphonia* (1988). The references are to Newman's edition. The remaining passages (*Scivias*, *The Book of Divine Works* and the rest of the *Letters*) were translated by Robert Carver (*SC* 1 14,16 and *DW* 4,78 have been slightly adapted by the editors). We are most grateful to all the translators for their efforts to render Hildegard's powerful but erratic Latin into modern English.

FB and OD

EXTRACTS FROM THE LIFE OF SAINT HILDEGARD
by Godfrey and Theodoric

Hildegard's childhood and the discovery of her visionary gifts

Wisdom teaches in the light of love, and bids me tell how I was brought into this my gift of vision . . . 'Hear these words, human creature, and tell them not according to yourself but according to me, and, taught by me, speak of yourself like this. – In my first formation, when in my mother's womb God raised me up with the breath of life, he fixed this vision in my soul. For, in the eleven hundredth year after Christ's incarnation, the teaching of the apostles and the burning justice which he had set in Christians and spiritual people began to grow sluggish and irresolute. In that period I was born, and my parents, amid sighs, vowed me to God. And in the third year of my life I saw so great a brightness that my soul trembled; yet because of my infant condition I could express nothing of it. But in my eighth year I was offered to God, given over to a spiritual way of life, and till my fifteenth I saw many things, speaking of a number of them in a simple way, so that those who heard me wondered from where they might have come or from whom they might be.

Then I too grew amazed at myself, that whenever I saw these things deep in my soul I still retained outer sight, and that I heard this said of no other human being. And, as best I could, I concealed the vision I saw in my soul. I was ignorant of much in the outer world, because of the frequent illness that I suffered, from the time of my mother's milk right up to now: it wore my body out and made my powers fail.

Exhausted by all this, I asked a nurse of mine if she saw anything save external objects. 'Nothing', she answered, for she saw none of those others. Then, seized with great fear, I did not dare reveal it to anyone; yet nonetheless, speaking or composing, I used to make many affirmations about future events, and when I was fully perfused by this vision I would say many things that were unfathomable (*aliena*) to whose who listened. But if the force of the vision – in which I made an exhibition of myself more childish than befitted my age – subsided a little, I blushed profusely and often wept, and many times I should gladly have kept silent, had I been allowed. And still, because of the fear I had of other people, I did not tell anyone *how* I saw. But a certain high-born woman, to whom I had been entrusted for education, noted this and disclosed it to a monk whom she knew.

. . . After her death, I kept seeing in this way till my fortieth year. Then in that same vision I was forced by a great pressure (*pressura*) of pains to manifest what I had seen and heard. But I was very much afraid, and blushed to utter what I had so long kept silent. However, at that time my veins and marrow became full of that strength which I had always lacked in my infancy and youth.

I intimated this to a monk who was my *magister* . . . Astonished, he bade me write these things down secretly, till he could see what they were and what their source might be. Then, realizing that they came from God, he indicated this to his abbot, and from that time on he worked at this [writing down] with me, with great eagerness.

In that same [experience of] vision I understood the writings of the prophets, the Gospels, the works of other holy men, and those of certain philosophers, without any human instruction, and I expounded certain things based on these, though I scarcely had literary understanding, inasmuch as a woman who was not learned had been my teacher. But I also brought forth songs with their melody, in praise of God and the saints, without being taught by anyone, and I sang them too, even though I had never learnt either musical notation or any kind of singing.

When these occurrences were brought up and discussed at

an audience in Mainz Cathedral, everyone said they stemmed from God, and from that gift of prophecy which the prophets of old had proclaimed. Then my writings were brought to Pope Eugene, when he was in Trier. With joy he had them read out in the presence of many people, and read them for himself, and, with great trust in God's grace, sending me his blessing with a letter, he bade me commit whatever I saw or heard in my vision to writing, more comprehensively than hitherto.'

B 6vb–7va
Dronke 145–6

Hildegard's move from Disibodenberg to Rupertsberg

At one time, because of a dimming of my eyes, I could see no light; I was weighed down in body by such a weight that I could not get up, but lay there assailed by the most intense pains. I suffered in this way because I had not divulged the vision I had been shown, that with my girls (*cum puellis meis*) I should move from the Disibodenberg, where I had been vowed to God, to another place. I was afflicted till I named the place where I am now. At once I regained my sight and had things easier, though I still did not recover fully from my sickness. But my abbot, and the monks and the populace in that province, when they realized what the move implied – that we wanted to go from fertile fields and vineyards and the loveliness of that spot to parched places where there were no amenities – were all amazed. And they intrigued so that this should not come about: they were determined to oppose us. What is more, they said I was deluded by some vain fantasy. When I heard this, my heart was crushed, and my body and veins dried up. Then, lying in bed for many days, I heard a mighty voice forbidding me to utter or to write anything more in that place about my vision.

Then a noble marchioness, who was known to us,

Extracts from the Life of Saint Hildegard | 65

approached the archbishop of Mainz and laid all this before him and before other wise counsellors. They said that no place could be hallowed except through good deeds, so that it seemed right that we should go ahead. And thus, by the archbishop's permission, with a vast escort of our kinsfolk and of other men, in reverence of God we came to the Rupertsberg. Then the ancient deceiver put me to the ordeal of great mockery, in that many people said: 'What's all this – so many hidden truths revealed to this foolish, unlearned woman, even though there are many brave and wise men around? Surely this will come to nothing!' For many people wondered whether my revelation stemmed from God, or from the parchedness (*inaquositas*) of aerial spirits, that often seduced human beings.

So I stayed in that place with twenty girls of noble and wealthy parentage, and we found no habitation or inhabitant there, save for one old man and his wife and children. Such great misfortunes and such pressure of toil befell me, it was as if a stormcloud covered the sun – so that, sighing and weeping copiously, I said: 'Oh, oh, God confounds no one who trusts in him!' Then God showed me his grace again, as when the clouds recede and the sun bursts forth, or when a mother offers her weeping child milk, restoring its joy after tears.

Then in true vision I saw that these tribulations had come to me according to the exemplar of Moses, for when he led the children of Israel from Egypt through the Red Sea into the desert, they, murmuring against God, caused great affliction to Moses too, even though God lit them on their way with wondrous signs. So God let me be oppressed in some measure by the common people, by my relatives, and by some of the women who had remained with me, when they lacked essential things (except inasmuch as, through God's grace, they were given to us as alms). For just as the children of Israel plagued Moses, so these people, shaking their heads over me, said: 'What good is it for well-born and wealthy girls to pass from a place where they lacked nothing into such penury?' But we were waiting for the grace of God, who had shown us this spot, to come to our aid.

After the pressure of such grief, he rained that bounty upon us. For many, who had previously despised us and called us a parched useless thing, came from every side to help us, filling us with blessings. And many rich people buried their dead on our land, with due honour . . .

Nonetheless, God did not want me to remain steadily in complete security: this he had shown me since infancy in all my concerns, sending me no carefree joy as regards this life, through which my mind could become overbearing. For when I was writing my book *Scivias*, I deeply cherished a nobly-born young girl, daughter of the marchioness I mentioned, just as Paul cherished Timothy. She had bound herself to me in loving friendship in every way, and showed compassion for my illnesses, till I had finished the book. But then, because of her family's distinction, she hankered after an appointment of more repute: she wanted to be named abbess of some splendid church. She pursued this not for the sake of God but for wordly honour. When she had left me, going to another region far away from us, she soon afterwards lost her life and the renown of her appointment.

Some other noble girls, too, acted in similar fashion, separating themselves from me. Some of them later lived such irresponsible lives that many people said, their actions showed that they sinned against the Holy Spirit, and against the person who spoke from out of the Spirit. But I and those who loved me wondered why such great persecution came upon me, and why God did not bring me comfort, since I did not wish to persevere in sins but longed to perfect good works with his help. Amid all this I completed my book *Scivias*, as God willed.

B 8va–9vb
Dronke 150–1

SCIVIAS
(Know the Ways of the Lord)

The receiving of the visions

In the year 1141 of the incarnation of Jesus Christ the Son of God, when I was forty two years and seven months of age, a fiery light, flashing intensely, came from the open vault of heaven and poured through my whole brain. Like a flame that is hot without burning it kindled all my heart and all my breast, just as the sun warms anything on which its rays fall. And suddenly I could understand what such books as the Psalter, the Gospel and the other catholic volumes both of the Old and New Testament actually set forth; but I could not interpret the words of the text; nor could I divide up the syllables; nor did I have any notion of the cases or tenses.

Ever since I was a girl – certainly from the time I was five years old right up to the present – in a wonderful way I had felt in myself (as I do even now) the strength and mystery of these secret and marvellous visions. Yet I revealed this to no one except for a very few people and the religious who lived in the same community as I; but right up until the time when God in his grace wished it to be revealed, I suppressed it beneath strict silence. The visions which I saw I did not perceive in dreams nor when asleep nor in a delirium nor with the eyes or ears of the body. I received them when I was awake and looking around with a clear mind, with the inner eyes and ears, in open places according to the will of God. But how this could be, it is difficult for us mortals to seek to know.

SC Introduction

Hildegard receives her visions

The writing of 'Scivias'

Although I saw and heard these things, nonetheless, because of doubt and mischievous rumour and the various things people said, for a long time (not out of obstinacy but through a sense of humility) I refused to write them until I fell upon my sick-bed, pressed down by the scourge of God. So at last, compelled by manifold infirmities, I set my hands to writing, having, as witnesses, a certain girl who was nobly-born and of good character and that man whom, as has been said before, I had sought out and found in secret.

While I was doing this, I sensed, as I said before, the deep profundity of what was being set forth in these books. Recovering my strength, I raised myself up from sickness and brought that work with difficulty to an end, devouring ten years in the process.

SC Introduction

The Spirit of God
gives life to the soul and
to the body

You see, as it were, a woman, who has in her womb the complete figure of a human being. This means that after the woman has received human seed a child is formed, perfect in all its parts, in the hidden chamber of her belly. And behold, through the secret plan of the supreme Creator, the same figure displays animated motion. For when, in accordance with the secret and hidden order and will of God, at an appropriate time rightly determined by divine providence, the child in its mother's womb has received the spirit, it shows by the movement of its body that it is alive. In the same way, the earth reveals itself and brings forth its crop of flowers when the dew has fallen upon it, just as *the fiery sphere (having none of the features of the human body) takes possession of that same figure's heart.* For the soul, blazing in the fire of profound knowledge, discerns various things in the orbit of its understanding. And, not having the form of human parts (since it is itself neither corporeal nor fallen like the human body), it greatly strengthens our heart because, being the foundation of the body, it rules the whole, just as the firmament of heaven contains the things below and protects the things above. The soul also affects the brain because, in its powers, it understands the things not only of earth but of heaven, when it knows God wisely. And it pours itself through all of our parts, since it has bestowed on the whole body the vigour of the marrow and of the veins and of all the limbs, just as the tree gives sap and greenness from the root to all its branches.

As it emerges from its mother, this same figure of a human being (which has been given life in this way) also changes colour, according to the motions which the sphere itself makes within it. For after we have received the life-giving spirit in our mother's womb, once

The Spirit of God gives life to the soul and to the body

we have been born in this way and begun to express ourselves in action, our own worth is apparent in terms of the works which the soul performs with the body. For we clothe ourselves with brightness from good things and with darkness from bad.

SC I 4, 16

The likeness of the soul to a tree

The soul is in the body as the sap is in the tree; and the powers of the soul are like the figure of the tree. How is this so? Understanding in the soul is like the green vigour of the branches and the leaves of the tree. Will is like the flowers on the tree; mind like the first fruit bursting forth. But reason is like the fruit in the fullness of maturity; while sense is like the height and spread of the tree. And in the same way, the human body is strengthened and supported by the soul.

SC I 4, 26

The Trinity

Just as the flame contains three essences in the one fire, so too, there is one God in three persons. How is this so? The flame consists of shining brightness, purple vigour and fiery glow. It has shining brightness so that it may give light; purple vigour so that it may flourish; and a fiery glow so that it may burn.

In the shining brightness, observe the Father who, in his fatherly devotion, reveals his brightness to the faithful. In the purple vigour contained within it (whereby this same flame manifests its power), understand the Son who, from the Virgin, assumed a body in which Godhead demonstrated its

The true unity of the Trinity

miracles. And in the fiery glow, perceive the Holy Spirit which pours glowingly into the minds of believers.

But where there is neither shining brightness, nor purple vigour, nor fiery glow, there no flame is seen. So too, where neither the Father nor the Son nor the Holy Spirit is honoured, there God is not worthily revered.

And so, just as these three essences are discerned in the one flame, so too, three Persons are to be understood in the unity of Godhead.

SC II 2, 6

On baptism

He who has believed and been baptized will be saved; but he who has not believed will be damned. What does this mean? That man who has seen through his understanding (which is the inner eye) what is hidden to external sight, and does not waver in this – he most certainly believes. *This* is faith. For what we perceive externally, we also know externally; and what we see internally, we also contemplate internally. So it is that when our understanding, looking ardently through the mirror of life, perceives the incomprehensible Godhead which the outer eye is unable to see, then the desires of the flesh are laid low and crushed to the ground.

Therefore, the spirit of that man sighs towards the true height. It feels the regeneration which was brought by the Son of Man. The Son of Man was conceived of the Holy Spirit. His Mother did not receive him in lust from the flesh of a sweating male, but from the secret part of the Father of all things. Coming in sweetness, he shows in the water the most pure and living mirror, so that through it man lives in regeneration.

For just as man is born from flesh, created by the divine power in the form of Adam, so the Holy Spirit restores the life of the soul through the pouring over of water. The water receives into itself the spirit of man as it rouses it to life, just as his spirit was revived previously in the wave of blood, when it was revealed in a vessel of flesh. For just as the form of man is fashioned through love, so that it is called 'man', so too, the spirit of man is given life in the water before the eyes of God, so that God acknowledges him in the inheritance of life.

So it is that he who accepts the fountain of deliverance with the covenant of Justice finds life in salvation because he faithfully believes. But he who does not wish to believe is dead, since he does not have the breath of the Holy Spirit on which to fly to the heights of heaven. Feeling his way with blind eyes, he trembles in the clouded understanding of the flesh, without being alive. For he lacks the life-enabling discipline which God has breathed into mankind to counteract the mounting will of the flesh.

SC II 3, 30

Against child oblates

'I have the green land under my control. Did I give that to you, man, so that you could make whatever crop you wanted germinate? And if you sow seed upon it surely you cannot induce it to fruit? No. For you can neither provide dew, nor produce rain, nor bestow moisture in greenness, nor draw heat with the glow of the sun – all of which are required for producing a crop.

'So, too, you can sow a word in a person's ear. But in the heart, which is my field, you can pour neither the dew of remorse, nor the rain of tears, nor the moistness of devotions, nor the warmth of the Holy Spirit – all of which are needed for the crop of holiness to germinate.

'And how did you dare so rashly to take hold of one dedicated and sanctified to me in baptism that you would hand him over against his will, to be bound in the most confining captivity to bear my yoke – when the result is neither parched nor green, so that he is neither dead to the world nor alive in it? And why have you oppressed him to such an extent that he is capable of neither? But that miracle of mine by which he must be strengthened in order to remain in the spiritual life is not to be examined by mortals. For I do not want the parents to sin in his consecration by offering him up to me against his will.

'But should some mother or father wish to offer their boy to my service, before presenting him, let that parent say: ''I promise God that I shall protect my boy with expert care until he reaches the age of reason, by imploring, beseeching, exhorting him to remain devotedly in the service of God. And if he is in agreement with me, I shall immediately offer his service to God; or if he does not give me his assent, I may be innocent in the eyes of God's majesty.''

'But if the parents of the boy have attended him in these ways until he has reached the age of reason; and if, at that stage, the same boy, turning away from them, does not wish to give his consent, then the parents themselves, since they have shown in him the strength of their devotion, should not offer him up against his will; nor should they force the boy into that service which they themselves are unwilling to bear or perform.'

SC II 5, 46

On the Eucharist

'*Eat, my friends, drink and get drunk, my dearest ones.* What does this mean? Eat in faith, you who have come to my friendship through holy baptism. For the pouring out of my Son's blood has wiped from you Adam's fall. Think upon the true remedy in the body of my Only-Begotten, so that the crimes you frequently repeat when you commit injustice in your works may be wiped mercifully from you. Drink in hope from this vine which has led you from eternal punishment. Take up the cup of salvation, so that you may believe firmly and courageously in that grace by which you have been redeemed. For you too will be drenched in that blood which was poured out for you. Become drunk with love, you who are most beloved of me. Be overflowing in the rivulets of the Scriptures, so that you tear yourselves away with the highest zeal from the desires of the flesh. Then I may kindle in you the dazzling virtues that are so lovely to me, as I hand over to you the body and blood of my Only-Begotten, just as he himself gave the same sacrament to his disciples, as is written in the Gospel.'

SC II 6, 21

The cup of life

'I want to declare marvellous things also in the wine which flows from the vine, by the same invocation through the sacrament of his blood.

'The blood of my Son flowed from his side, just as the grape drips from the vine. But just as the grape is trodden by feet and crushed in the press, with the sweetest and strongest wine flowing out to strengthen the blood in man, so too, in my Only-Begotten, in the sweat of his distress, as he was bruised by blows and scourges, crushed by the timber of the cross, the excellent and most precious blood flowed from his wounds, drenching in salvific deliverance the people who believed . . .

'. . . For just as the wine drips from the vine, so too, my Son issued from my heart. My Only-Begotten is the true vine – with shoots issuing from him in different directions. For the faithful have been planted in him and through his incarnation they abound in the fruit of good works.

'And as that juice flows from the sweetest and strongest fruit of the vine, so too all justice appears in mercy and truth through the incarnation of my Son. All those who faithfully seek these virtues, discover them in him. How is this so? Those who faithfully cling to him are made green and fruitful by him so that in these virtues they bear excellent fruit. In the same way, being sweet and gentle, he brought forth the most precious buds in holiness and justice and those who believed in him, he cleansed of all the dirt of unfaithfulness.'

SC II 6, 28

A call for renewal

'Those who willingly endure poverty in my name are truly worthy of my love; while those who through their greed would gladly have worldly riches, but are not able to have them, lose the profit of their labour. Yet he who seeks riches to satisfy in them my will and not his greed, will have in my house the reward of glory for his good will.

'So too, he who seeks the power of glory because of his bragging arrogance and not for the glory of my name – seems to me like a stinking corpse. But he who seeks glory for the sake not of his own arrogance but of my renown, will appear full of glory in my Kingdom.

'For this reason, priests ought to submit to the teaching of their spiritual office's rule not for themselves but for me, so that they may be able to preside over my people so much more steadfastly and devoutly.'

SC II 6, 92

The two paths

'Man has within him two callings – a desire for success and a longing for failure. How is this so? Through the desire for success, he is called to life. Through the longing for failure he is called to death. When, in the longing for success, man desires to do good, saying to himself, "Perform good works", this is a response against evil – to avoid it and produce useful fruit. But when, in the longing for failure, he desires to commit evil, urging himself on in this way: "Do whatever gives you pleasure", this is a response against good, since he does not wish to resist his own iniquity, but delights in achieving failure. He shows his contempt for me in this response and reckons me a trickster by not bestowing the honour due to me.'

SC III 5, 6

Chastity

The seventh figure represents Chastity. For once people have placed their hope fully in God, the work grows to perfection within them, so that they begin in chastity to restrain themselves from fleshly desires. Chastity, in the flower of the flesh, feels abstinence most keenly, just as a young maiden feels the glow of desire, yet does not attempt to look back at a man.

In this way, Chastity casts aside all that is unclean, panting with glorious desires towards her delightful lover. He is the sweetest and loveliest essence of all good things amongst the delights of all the powers which stem from constancy; and he can be perceived by his lovers only with the inner beauty of the soul.

For this reason, Chastity is clothed in a tunic, purer, more full of light than crystal. It shines with a brilliance like the glittering of water drenched with sun. For she is dazzling in her single purpose, and utterly clean of any of the dust of concupiscence's burning lust. She is wonderfully strengthened through the Holy Spirit and has been clothed in the robe of innocence. Her robe shines in the dazzling whiteness of the fountain of living water which is the brilliant sun of eternal brightness.

Above her head, turned towards her face, stands a dove, its wings stretched as though for flight. This signifies that, from the outset, Chastity was cherished by the expanse and shading of the wings – that is, by the protection of the Holy Spirit – which enabled her to fly through the twists and turns of the devil's snares. She sees her way by means of the fiery love of holy inspiration, guiding herself towards the place where she reveals the countenance of her sweetness.

SC III 8, 24

Divine Wisdom

You see a figure of great beauty standing on the top of this floor. This means that this virtue was in the Father on high 'before all creation', arranging in his judgement all the materials of creation established in heaven and on earth. She herself, it is clear, shines in him as a great adornment, being the broadest step amongst the steps of the other virtues in him. She is joined to him in a dance, in the sweetest embrace of blazing love.

Wisdom looks towards the people on the earth. For she always rules and defends with her protection those who try to follow her, loving them greatly because they are steadfast in her. For that same figure signifies the Wisdom of God: since, through her, all things were created and are ruled by God. *Her head shines like lightning: with such brightness that you cannot have your fill of gazing upon it.* For the Godhead is both terrible and enticing to all creation, seeing and contemplating all things, just as the human eye discerns what is placed before it. Yet no mortal can ultimately comprehend the Godhead, in all the profundity of its mystery.

Wisdom arranges her hands reverently upon her breast. This signifies the power of Wisdom which she wisely restrains, so that she directs every work of hers in such a way that no one can resist her, either in prudence or power.

Her feet on the same floor, are hidden from your sight. For her way, concealed in the heart of the Father, lies open to no mortal. Her secrets are naked and manifest to God alone. *She has on her head a ring in the form of a crown, shining with great brilliance.* This signifies that the majesty of God, being without beginning or end, shines with an incomparable glory, God-head radiating with such splendour that mortal minds are overwhelmed. As for her being clothed in a tunic the colour of gold; this signifies that the work of Wisdom is frequently considered as though it were the purest gold. For this reason, *she is adorned with a belt that descends from her breast right down to her feet, decorated with most precious jewels and glittering in a brilliant play of green and white and red and sky-blue.* For, from the beginning of the world, when Wisdom first displayed her work openly, she already extended as far as the end of the world, like a single path, adorned with holy and just commands, that is to say, with the first planting of the green seed of the patriarchs and of the prophets who, in wretched lamentation for their suffering, entreated with such great desire for the Son of God to be made flesh. Then she was graced with the dazzling virginity of the Virgin Mary; next, with the solid and ruddy faith of the martyrs; and finally with the brilliant and light-filled love of contemplation, by which God and neighbour ought to be loved through the heat of the Holy Spirit.

She will go on in this way until the end of the world, and her warning will not cease but will flow out always, as long as the world endures.

SC III 9, 25

Spiritual music

Just as the power of God, extending everywhere, surrounds all things without encountering any resistance, so too, the rationality of man has the great ability to sound through living voices and to rouse listless souls to wakefulness in music.

Even David demonstrates this in the music of his prophecy and Jeremiah shows it in the sorrowful voice of his lamentation. *So it is that even you – a poor, weak-natured little woman – hear, in music, the sound of fiery ardour in the virgin's blush, in the embracing words of the budding twig; the sound of keenness from the living lights that shine in the celestial city; the sound of prophecy in deep sermons; the sound of marvellous words from the enlarging of the apostleship; the sound of blood being poured out by those who offer themselves up in faith; the sound of the priestly mysteries being observed; and the sound of the virgin's step on the heavenly greenness of flowering things.* For faithful creation echoes back to the heavenly Creator with its voice of exultation and joy, returning frequent thanks. *But you also hear a sound like the voice of a great throng, resounding in harmony in the complaints of those recalled to the same steps.* For music not only rejoices in the unanimity of exultation of those who bravely persevere along the path of righteousness. It also exults in the concord of reviving those who have fallen away from the path of justice and are lifted up at last to blessedness. For even the good shepherd joyfully led back to the flock the sheep that had been lost.

SC III 13, 13

Musical harmony softens hard hearts

Musical harmony softens hard hearts, inducing in them the moisture of contrition and summoning the Holy Spirit. So it is that those voices that you hear are like the voice of the multitude when they lift up their voices on high. For the faithful carry their jubilant praises in the singleness of unanimity and revealed love, towards that unity of mind where there is no discord, when they make those on earth sigh with hearts and mouths for their heavenly reward.

And the sound of those voices passes through you in such a way that you understand them without being hindered by dullness. For whatever divine grace has been at work, it removes all shadow of obscurity, making those things pure and full of light that had been concealed by the carnal senses in the weakness of the flesh.

SC III 13, 14

THE BOOK OF LIFE'S MERITS

Hardness of heart and mercy

The fourth vision gathered like a cloud of thick smoke and took on human form, but without arms or legs – only huge black eyes that stared unblinking. Perfectly still, it remained out there in the dark, motionless. It spoke:

HARDNESS OF HEART: I have produced nothing and brought no one into existence. So why should I bother about anything? I intend to leave things as they are and only help people when they are useful to me. God created everything; let him take care of it all! If I became involved, even just a little, in other people's affairs, what use would it do me? And even if I did, I would do them neither good nor harm. I could go around feeling pity for everyone and everything, but I wouldn't get a moment's peace; and what would become of me? What kind of life would I lead if I had to find an answer for every voice of joy or sadness? I know only that I myself exist; and everyone else should do the same.

Again I heard a voice from the cloud. It spoke:

MERCY'S REPLY: What are you saying, you creature of stone? The plants give off the fragrance of their flowers. The precious stones reflect their brilliance to others. Every creature yearns for a loving embrace. The whole of nature serves humanity, and in this service offers all her bounty. But you have not even merited full human form. All you are is a pitiless stare, an evil cloud of smoke in the darkness!

But I am soothing herb. I dwell in the dew and in the air and in all greenness. My heart fills to overflowing and I give help to others. I was there when the first words resounded: 'Let there be'. From these words the whole of creation issued forth which stands today at the disposal of humanity. But you are excluded. With a loving eye, I observe the demands of life and feel myself a part of all. I lift up the broken-hearted and lead them to wholeness, since I am the balm for every pain, and since my words ring true while you remain what you are: a bitter cloud of smoke!

LM 1, 16–17

The sin of those who think they were born to be unhappy

As soon as some people find themselves faced with the vicissitudes of everyday life, they start to mistrust God. They decide that they must be fated to be unhappy.

'God does not want to help us', they claim, 'and he can't do so either. We are stuck with the life of misery we were born into, and there is no escape.'

People who say such things in their hearts should turn and place all their trust in God's mercy. In their longing for higher things, they should confess their failure so that they can still merit God's grace. For human beings are by nature good. It is their own fault if they pervert their true natures and give full rein to their arbitrary desires.

These words concern penitent people, whose souls can still be purified and saved; and they are true. Let the faithful take care to keep this firmly fixed in the memory of their good conscience.

LM 2, 93

The vice of forgetting about God

Forgetting about God leads to harmful thoughts and idle chatter such as: 'How can we know about God if we have never seen him? And why should we have any regard for him if we have never set eyes on him?' People who talk like that are no longer mindful of their Creator, and their minds are smothered in the darkness of unbelief. For when man fell, darkness fell on the whole of creation. But God had created human beings to be full of light so that they could see the radiance of pure ether and hear the songs of angels. He had clothed them in such radiance that they shone with the splendour of it. But all this was lost when man disobeyed God's commandment and so caused nature to fall with him. Yet the natural elements retained a glimmering of their former pristine position, which human sin could not destroy completely. For which reason people should retain a glimmering of their knowledge of God. They should allow God to return to the centre of their lives, recognizing that they owe their very existence to no one else save God alone, who is the Creator of all.

LM 4, 67

The heavenly joy of the virgins

Again in that light, as in a mirror, I saw a layer of air, pure beyond the clarity of the purest water. It shone with light, stronger than the rays of the sun. It had life and it contained the vital force of all the herbs and flowers of earth and paradise, filled with the fragrance of life-giving power, just as the summer is filled with the scent of green plants and flowers. As though in a mirror, I saw in that layer of air those blessed women, clothed in gowns of purest gold. From the chest to the feet they were adorned with precious jewels, in the manner of a woman's hanging girdle. They too were as fragrant as sweet-smelling herbs. And their belts were decorated with gold and pearls and delicate workmanship beyond the limits of human conception.

On their heads they wore golden crowns studded with gems and interwoven with roses and lilies. Whenever the voice of the Lamb resounded, a breath of wind sprang up from the depths of the Godhead which stirred the stems of the roses and lilies till they rang out like the strings of harps; a wonderful music was heard, in perfect harmony with the voice of the Lamb. Only they who wore the crowns could sing this music, and only they could hear the song, rejoicing in it, as they delight who first set their eyes on the sun's unimagined splendour.

Their shoes shone with light like a spring of living water. At times they seemed to hover, as on golden wheels. Again they took up their harps and again that wonderful music rang out. They began to speak a strange unearthly language that no one else could speak or understand. As to the rest of their radiance – that was beyond the power of my eyes to see.

Because during their bodily existence these women had achieved a real faith in God their Creator, and had performed good works, they found themselves in the joy and serenity of that glorious splendour I have just described. By their purity of purpose, they have overcome their vain, empty, unpredictable desires. Through their passionate love for the true sun, they had ascended to that level beyond the confines of prescribed laws and now they could breathe a new air, an air pure beyond the clarity of the purest water; and they shone with a radiance beyond the radiant glory of the sun. In the green life of their virginity and in the blossoming of body and spirit, these women had revealed the sweetest longings. Inspired by the Holy Spirit, they had been filled with the fragrance and power of many virtues. And now they could feel the breath of a new air, air that breathes the fresh green force of all the herbs and flowers of earth and paradise; air that is filled with the fragrance of life-giving power, just as the summer is filled with the scent of green plants and flowers.

They followed the way of life of God's incarnate Son and their hearts soared to great heights. They vowed to God to preserve their virginity in awe and sacred worship. So now, rejoicing with them, the Lamb of God lifts up his voice. A sweet breath of wind, rising from the depths of God, touches these emblems of their crowned virginity so that they start to join in the song of the Lamb, a music unknown to those who do not possess such emblems but who are overjoyed when they finally hear it. And because they trod the path taken by God when he became man by ancient design, their shoes shone with such a light so that it was as if they had been taken from a spring of living water.

LM 6, 43–6, 48

THE BOOK OF DIVINE WORKS

Hildegard's commission

For five years I had been troubled by true and wonderful visions. For a true vision of the unfailing light had shown me (in my great ignorance) the diversity of various ways of life. In the sixth year (which marked the beginning of the present visions), when I was sixty-five years of age, I saw a vision of such mystery and power that I trembled all over and – because of the frailty of my body – began to sicken. It was only after seven years that I finally finished writing down this vision. And so, in the year of our Lord's incarnation, 1163, when the apostolic throne was still being oppressed by the Roman Emperor, Frederick, a voice came to me from heaven, saying:

> O poor little figure of a woman; you, who are the daughter of many troubles, plagued by a grave multitude of bodily infirmities, yet steeped, nonetheless, in the vastness of God's mysteries – commit to permanent record for the benefit of humankind, what you see with your inner eyes and perceive with the inner ears of your soul so that, through these things, people may come to know their Creator and not recoil from worshipping him with the reverence due to him. And so, write these things, not according to your heart but according to my witness – for I am Life without beginning or end. These things were not devised by you, nor were they previously considered by anyone else; but they were pre-ordained by me before the beginning of the world. For just as I had foreknowledge of man before he was made, so too I foresaw all that he would need.

And so I, a poor and feeble little figure of a woman, set my hands to the task of writing – though I was worn down by so many illnesses, and trembling. All this was witnessed by that man [Volmar] whom (as I explained in my earlier visions) I had sought and found in secret, as well as by that girl [Richardis] whom I mentioned in the same context.

While I was doing this, I looked up at the true and living light to see what I ought to write. For everything which I had written since the beginning of my visions (or which I came to understand afterwards) I saw with the inner eyes of my spirit and heard with my inner ears, in heavenly mysteries, fully awake in body and mind – and not in dreams, nor in ecstasy, as I explained in my previous visions. Nor (as truth is my witness) did I produce anything from the faculty of the human sense, but only set down those things which I perceived in heavenly mysteries.

And again I heard a voice from heaven instructing me thus; and it said: 'Write in this way, just as I tell you.'

DW Foreword

The source of all being

'I, the highest and fiery power, have kindled every living spark and I have breathed out nothing that can die. But I determine how things are – I have regulated the circuit of the heavens by flying around its revolving track with my upper wings – that is to say, with Wisdom. But I am also the fiery life of the divine essence – I flame above the beauty of the fields; I shine in the waters; in the sun, the moon and the stars, I burn. And by means of the airy wind, I stir everything into quickness with a certain invisible life which sustains all. For the air lives in its green power and its blossoming; the waters flow as if they were alive. Even the sun is alive in its own light; and when the moon is on the point of disappearing, it is kindled by the sun, so that it lives, as it were, afresh. I have also set up the pillars that sustain the orb of the earth, as well as those winds which have subordinate wings (that is to say, gentler winds) which, through their mildness, hold the stronger winds in check, so that they do not prove a danger. In the same way, the body covers and encloses the soul so that it does not rush out.

For just as the breathing of the soul holds the body together by supporting it, so that it does not fail, so too the strong winds animate the subordinate winds so that they function as they should. And so I, the fiery power, lie hidden in these things and they blaze from me, just as man is continually moved by his breath, and as the fire contains the nimble flame. All these things live in their own essence and are without death, since I am Life. I am also rationality, having the wind of the resounding Word (through which all creation was made) and I have breathed into all these things, so that there is nothing mortal in their natures, because I am Life itself. For I am the whole of life – life was not torn from stones; it did not bud from branches; nor is it rooted in the generative power of the male. Rather, every living thing is rooted in me. For rationality is the root, but the resounding Word flowers in it.

Hence, since God is rational, how could he not be at work, since all his work blossoms in man whom he made in his own image and likeness and in whom he expressed all creation according to fixed measure. For it was always the case throughout eternity that God wanted his work, man, to come into being. And when he finished the task, he gave man all the creatures so that he might work with them, just as God had made man as his own work.

But I am also of service since all living things take their radiance from me; and I am the life which remains the same through eternity, having neither beginning nor end; and the same life, working and moving itself is God and yet this life is one in three powers. And so Eternity is called the Father, the Word is called the Son and the breath that connects these two is called the Holy Spirit; just as God marked it in man in whom there are body, soul and rationality.

But the fact that I flame above the beauty of the fields signifies the earth, which is the stuff from which God made man. And my shining in the waters accords with the soul; because just as the water pours over the whole earth, so the soul pervades the whole body. That I glow in the sun and the moon, signifies rationality; but the stars are the countless words of rationality. And the fact that by means of the airy wind I stir everything into quickness with a certain invisible life which sustains all, signifies this: those things which advance in growth are animated and sustained by the air and wind and remain quite unchanged in their essence.'

DW 1, 2

The love of the righteous

The King has brought me into his store-rooms. We shall exult and rejoice in you, mindful of your richness beyond the wine. The righteous love you (Song of Sol. 1).

This may be understood as follows: Because I, the soul of a faithful individual, have followed the Son of God (who has redeemed mankind through his humanity) along the path of truth, he, who is the ruler of all things, has brought me into the fulness of his gifts. There I find every abundance of virtues. I climb in faith from one virtue to the next. So it is that all of us who have been redeemed through the Son of God's blood will exult with our whole body and rejoice with our whole soul in you, O holy Godhead. Through you we exist, and we call to mind the sweetness of heavenly rewards more than all the agonies and trials which we have suffered at the hands of the enemies of truth, so that we reckon them as nothing, while we taste the delights which you extend in the display of your commandments. And so those who are righteous in the works of holiness love you with a true and perfect love, because you grant all good things to those who love you, even, in the end, bestowing upon them eternal life.

But Wisdom also pours into the store-rooms (that is, into the minds of mortals), and deposits the justice of true faith through which the true God is known. There, the same faith so checks the winter and damp of vices that they have no means of further bloom or growth; and it draws and unites with itself all the virtues, just as wine is poured into a vessel and given to people to drink. For this reason, the faithful, exulting and rejoicing in true confidence in their eternal reward, carry the bundles of good works they have performed. They thirst for God's Justice and they suck holiness from her breasts. Nor can they be satiated in any way, since they always delight in contemplation of the divine; for holiness passes all human understanding. For when man receives righteousness, he surrenders himself and tastes and drinks virtues, and through these he is strengthened, just as the veins of someone drinking are filled with wine. Yet he is neither unbridled in the vices of unfaithfulness nor a servant to them – unlike the drunkard who is beyond himself on account of the wine and pays no heed to what he is doing.

So the righteous love God, because they find in him no source of weariness, only an enduring blessedness.

DW 2, 19

The wheel of life

The firmament has a revolving orbit in imitation of the power of God which has neither beginning nor end – just as no one can see where the encircling wheel begins or ends. For the throne of God is his eternity in which he alone sits, and all the living sparks are rays of his splendour, just as the rays of the sun proceed from the sun itself.

The wheel of life

And how could God be known to be life, except through the living things which glorify him, since the things that praise his glory have proceeded from him? For this reason, he placed the living and burning sparks to brighten his face. These sparks see that he has neither beginning nor end and (unable to have their fill of gazing at him), they look eagerly upon him without satiety, with a zeal that can never diminish. But how could he, who is alone immortal, be known if the angels did not gaze upon him in this way? If he did not have those sparks, how could his full glory be apparent? And how could he be known to be eternal, if no brightness proceeded from him? For there is nothing in creation that does not have some radiance – either greenness or seeds or flowers, or beauty – otherwise it would not be part of creation. For if God were not able to make all things, where would be his power?

DW 4, 11

The work of the soul in the body

The soul assists the flesh and the flesh, the soul. For every single work is perfected through soul as well as flesh, so that the soul is revived by doing good and holy works with the flesh. But the flesh is often irked when co-operating with the soul, and so the soul stoops to the level of the flesh and allows it to take delight in some deed, just as a mother causes her weeping child to laugh. And in this way, the flesh performs some good works with the soul, but mixed together with certain sins which the soul tolerates so that the flesh is not oppressed. For just as the flesh lives through the soul, so too, the soul is revived by doing good works with the flesh, because the soul has been stationed inside the work of the Lord's hands. In the same way that the sun, overcoming night, climbs until the middle of the day, so man, too, rises up, by avoiding corrupt deeds. And just as the sun declines in the afternoon, so too, the soul makes accord with the flesh. And as the moon is rekindled by the sun so that it does not disappear, so the flesh of man is sustained by the powers of the soul, so that it does not go to ruin.

DW 4, 24

The stages of life are like the seasons of the earth

Human beings reach perfection in the flowering of childhood and early adulthood. Then in old age they go into withered decline, just as in summer the earth is adorned as it blossoms in greenness, and then in winter turns pale with the cold. For when the soul has so overcome the body that it accords with it in simple heart and good will, and is delighted with good works as though with some delicious food, that person says in heavenly desire, 'How sweet are the declarations of your justice in my throat. To my mouth, too, they are far sweeter than honey.' And so with a child's simplicity, that person lives in innocence, without fleshly desire. But the soul so steeps that one in these desires that he grows green as he climbs from virtue to virtue, and blossoms in the good works and examples that the Son of God has left us. For being untainted by the malice of sins, that person rejoices within and is adorned. And just as in the cold of winter, the greenness, blossoming and maturing of all the fruits fail, so in death human beings fail in all their works, both good and bad. But the person who, in infancy, childhood and old age has completed good works happily – his soul, shining with these same works and, as it were, adorned with precious stones, climbs into the presence of God; and the body, which performed these works through the soul, can scarcely wait until they abide together in the mansion of joy.

DW 4, 78

The life which endures

My days have declined away like a shadow and I am like the grass in the field (Psalm 102.11). This can be understood in the following way: Because of original sin, man is blind to what has passed and what is to come, so that his understanding of these things is like a shadow. On this account too, he lacks stability, just as the grass withers, since all that he does is unclear to him. For all of man's days are led into oblivion by this decline; but the life that is eternal is unchanging yet ever-fresh, just as the summer brings forth new fruits each year.

DW 4, 89

God is life in its fullness

And so God, who made all the things which have been mentioned previously, is the unique life from which all life takes its breath, just as a ray comes from the sun; and he is the fire from which every fire that looks towards blessedness is kindled, just as sparks emerge from fire. And how could it be appropriate if no living thing clung to this life and no fire warmed or illuminated any life? And how could it be fitting if no life or brightness proceeded from the Godhead, which was life before time? And what good would it do if the light kindled from this fire shone on no one, since the fire does not hide its light, nor the sun its ray? For God is that life through which the host of angels was kindled, like sparks leaping from a fire. So it would be inappropriate if this life did not shine forth. And that brightness is unfailing since in it there can be no death. How is this so? God alone exists through and in himself and did not receive his being from anyone else. But everything else in creation takes its beginning from him.

DW 5, 14

The fountain of life

I also saw, as if in the middle of the southern region I mentioned, three figures, two of whom were standing in a fountain of great purity, which was surrounded by a round stone, pierced with holes. They seemed to be rooted in it, just as trees sometimes appear to be growing in water. One was clad in purple, the other in white, but of such a brightness that I could not look at them directly. The third, however, was standing out of the fountain, on the stone. She was clad in a white robe, and her face shone with such radiance that my face flinched from it. And the blessed ranks of saints appeared like clouds before them and they gazed intently upon them.

DW 8, 1

Love speaks

But now the first figure began to speak: 'I am Love – the radiance of the living God. Wisdom has performed her work with me, and Humility (who is rooted in the living fountain) is my helper. To her, Peace clings. And through the brightness that I am, the living light of the blessed angels blazes. For, just as a ray flashes from a lamp, so this brightness shines in the blessed angels – nor could it do otherwise, since a light cannot help but shine. For I designed man, who was rooted in me like a reflected image, just as the semblance of each thing is seen in

The fountain of life

the water. So too, I am the living fountain because all the things that have been made were like a reflection in me. Man was made with fire and water according to this reflection, just as I am the fire and the living water. For this reason, man has it in his soul to arrange everything according to his will.'

DW 8, 2

Wisdom reveals her works through Hildegard

Wisdom contemplated her own work, which she had arranged in proper order in the reflection of the living water, when she revealed through that aforementioned unlearned figure of a woman, certain natural virtues of various things and certain writings about the life of merits, and certain other deep mysteries which that same woman saw in a true vision and which exhausted her.

DW 8, 2

The purity of the living God

'The leaping fountain is clearly the purity of the living God. His radiance is reflected in it, and in that splendour, God embraces in his great love all things whose reflection appeared in the leaping fountain before he ordered them to come forth in their own shape. And in me, Love, all things are reflected and my splendour reveals the design of things, just as the reflection indicates their form. In Humility, who is my helper, creation came forth at God's command; and in that same Humility, God inclined himself towards me, to lift up again through that blessedness (through which he can do all that he will) the withered leaves that had fallen. For he fashioned them out of the earth; and from the earth he freed them after the fall.'

DW 8, 2

Love, Humility and Peace

Everything that God has effected, he has perfected in Love, Humility and Peace. So it is, that man, too, should esteem Love, embrace Humility and grasp Peace, lest he rush into destruction along with the one who has been mocking those virtues from the moment of his birth.

DW 8, 3

Love leads humanity to the marriage of the King

For man is the work of the right hand of God. Through God he was clothed and called to the royal marriage which Humility made when God looked down from his lofty height into the depths of the earth and assembled his Church from the whole people. So it was that man, who had fallen, could climb again through repentance and renew himself in the ways of holiness and the different virtues, as though adorned with the greenness of flowers. But Arrogance is always corrupt – for she oppresses, divides and alienates every single thing, while Humility does not steal from anyone and alienates nothing. Rather, she maintains everything in Love. In her, God stoops towards the earth. Through her, he gathers together all the virtues. For the virtues stretch towards the Son of God, just as a virgin, disdaining a husband of flesh, calls Christ her bridegroom. And these virtues are joined to Humility when she leads them to the marriage of the King.

DW 8, 4

The goodness of all created things

God's works are so secured by an all-encompassing plenitude, that no created thing is imperfect. It lacks nothing in its nature, possessing in itself the fullness of all perfection and utility.

And so all things which came forth through Wisdom, remain in her like a most pure and elegant adornment, and they shine with the most splendid radiance of their individual essence.

And when fulfilling the precepts of God's commandments, man, too, is the sweet and dazzling robe of Wisdom. He serves as her green garment through his good intentions and the green vigour of works adorned with virtues of many kinds. He is an ornament to her ears when he turns away from hearing evil whispers; a protection for her breast, when he rejects forbidden desires. His bravery gives glory to her arms, too, when he defends himself against sin. For all of these things arise from the purity of faith, adorned with the profound gifts of the Holy Spirit and the most just writings of the Doctors of the Church, when man has perfected them in faith through good works.

DW 9, 2

God's judgement will fall upon priests who despoil the Church

After Justice has brought her accusation before the Supreme Judge, hearing her cries of complaint, he will, by his just judgement, allow his vengeance to rage against the transgressors of righteousness; and the enemies of God and Justice will have their tyranny turned upon themselves, while God and Justice say in turn: 'How long will we suffer and endure these ravening wolves, who ought to be physicians and are not?'

But because they have the power of preaching, imposing penance and granting absolution, for that reason, they hold us in their grasp like ferocious beasts. Their crimes fall upon us and through them the whole Church withers, because they do not proclaim what is just; and they destroy the law like wolves devouring sheep. They are voracious in their drunkenness and they commit copious adulteries, and because of such sins, they judge us without mercy.

For they are also plunderers of their congregations, through their avarice, devouring whatever they can; and with their offices they reduce us to poverty and indigence, contaminating both themselves and us. For this reason, let us judge and single them out in a fair trial, because they lead us astray rather than teaching us what is right. We should do this so that we are not destroyed, since if they persevere in this way, they will throw the whole land into confusion by bringing it under their sway. But now, let us tell them to fulfil the obligations of their priestly habit and office according to true religion, as the ancient Fathers established them, or depart from us and leave us what they have.

Spurred on by the divine decree, the people will angrily propose to them these and similar things, and overwhelming them will say, 'We do not want them to rule over us along with the estates and fields and other secular concerns over which we have been established as princes'.

And how can it be right that the shaven-headed with their robes and chasubles should have more soldiers and more weapons than we do? Surely too, it is inappropriate for a cleric to be a soldier or a soldier a cleric? So let us take away from them what is not fairly but unjustly theirs. But we should give careful consideration to what was offered up with great discernment for the souls of the departed, and leave that to them since it does not constitute plunder.

For the Almighty Father has rightly divided all things – heaven for heavenly things, earth for earthly things. In this way there is a just division among the sons of men, that the religious have those things which relate to them, while the laity have their own portion, so that neither party should oppress the other through acts of plundering. God indeed has not decreed that the tunic and cloak should be given to one son while the other remains naked, but has ordered that the cloak should be given to one, the tunic to the other. And so let the laity have the cloak, because of the bulk of their worldly concerns and on account of their offspring who are always growing and multiplying. But let the tunic be given to the religious population, so that they lack neither food nor clothing, but do not possess more than they need.

DW 10, 16

Epilogue: through her infirmities, Hildegard becomes the dwelling-place of the Holy-Spirit

And again I heard a voice from heaven teaching me these words:

Now, praise be to God in his work, man. For his restoration, God caused mighty battles on the earth and he deigned to raise him above the heavens so that, with the angels, he praises his face in that unity in which there is true God and true man. May Almighty God himself deign to anoint with the oil of his pity this poor little figure of a woman through whom he produced what is written here. For she lives devoid of all security, lacking even a knowledge of the structure of the Scriptures which the Holy Spirit set up for the instruction of the Church – the Scriptures which are like the wall of a great city.

Since the day of her birth, she has been entangled, as though in a net, in the afflictions of her infirmities, so that she is troubled by continual pains in all her veins, marrow and flesh. It has not, however, been God's will that she be released since, through the cavern of the rational soul, she sees, in a spiritual sense, some of the mysteries of God. But this vision so courses through her veins that frequently she is affected by great fatigue. Sometimes she is affected quite mildly; at other times, more seriously, when she is brought to exhaustion by her illness. For this reason, she maintains a way of life far removed from the various lifestyles of others; like a child whose veins are not yet full enough to enable it to discern the way people live.

For with the inspiration of the Holy Spirit, she lives in service, and she takes her physical constitution from the air. This infirmity is so impressed on her – from the air itself, from the rain, from the wind, from every sort of weather – that she can place no reliance on her flesh. Yet were it otherwise, the inspiration of the Holy Spirit would be unable to dwell within her.

But from time to time, the Spirit of God, in the mighty power of his holiness, revives her from the deathly extremes of this sickness with, as it were, the cool dew of consolation, so that she can live in service in the world with the inspiration of the Holy Spirit. But may Almighty God, who knows in truth all the weariness of this person's suffering, so deign to perfect his grace in her that his holiness may be glorified in this; and when her soul has migrated from this world to the eternal glory, it may rejoice at being received mercifully and being crowned.

But the Book of Life (which is the written expression of the Word of God – the Word through which all creation appeared; the Word which breathed forth the life of all things according to the will of the Eternal Father as he had pre-ordained them in himself) miraculously produced what is written here – not through any teaching of human knowledge, but through the simple and untaught figure of a woman.

Let no one, therefore, be so presumptuous as to add anything to the words of what is written here or take anything away, on pain of being erased from the Book of Life and from all the blessedness under the sun, unless this be done as a result of the copying of the letters and words which were brought forth directly through the inspiration of the Holy Spirit. Whoever presumes to do otherwise, sins against the Holy Spirit and will not be forgiven in this world or the next.

Now again, praise be to Almighty God in all his works before time and in time, since he is the First and the Last. But may the faithful regard these words with devout affection of heart since they were produced through him who is the First and Last for the benefit of believers.

DW Epilogue, 38

CAUSES AND CURES

The four elements

That there are only four elements: There cannot be more than four, or fewer. They consist of two kinds: upper and lower. The upper are celestial, the lower terrestrial. The things that live in the upper ones are impalpable and are made of fire and air; those that move in the lower are palpable, formed bodies, and consist of water and mud.

For spirits are fiery and airy, but man is watery and muddy. When God created man, the mud from which he was formed was stuck together with water, and God put a fiery and airy breath of life into that form.

Dronke 174, 242–3; Kaiser 41–5

Adam and Eve

When God created Adam, Adam experienced a sense of great love in the sleep that God instilled in him. And God gave a form to that love of the man, and so woman is the man's love. And as soon as woman was formed God gave man the power of creating, that through his love – which is woman – he might procreate children. When Adam gazed at Eve, he was entirely filled with wisdom, for he saw in her the mother of the children to come. And when she gazed at Adam, it was as if she were gazing into heaven, or as the human soul strives upwards, longing for heavenly things – for her hope was fixed in him. And so there will be and must be one and the same love in man and woman, and no other.

The man's love, compared with the woman's, is a heat of

ardour like a fire on blazing mountains, which can hardly be put out, whilst hers is a wood-fire that is easily quenched; but the woman's love, compared with the man's, is like a sweet warmth proceeding from the sun, which brings forth fruits.

But the great love that was in Adam when Eve came forth from him, and the sweetness of the sleep with which he then slept, were turned in his transgression into a contrary mode of sweetness. And so, because a man still feels this great sweetness in himself, and is like a stag thirsting for the fountain, he races swiftly to the woman and she to him – she like a threshing-floor pounded by his many strokes and brought to heat when the grains are threshed inside her.

Dronke 176, 244; Kaiser 136–7

The four temperaments of woman

(*De sanguinea*) Some women are inclined to plumpness, and have soft and delectable flesh and slender veins, and well-constituted blood free of impurities . . . And these have a clear and light colouring, and in love's embraces are themselves lovable; they are subtle in arts, and show self-restraint in their disposition. At menstruation they suffer only a moderate loss of blood, and their womb is well developed for childbearing, so they are fertile and can take in the man's seed. Yet they do not bear many children, and if they are without husbands, so that they remain childless, they easily have physical pains; but if they have husbands, they are well.

(*De flecmatica*) There are other women whose flesh does not develop as much, because they have thick veins and healthy, whitish blood (though it does contain a little impurity, which is the source of its light colour). They have severe features, and are darkish in colouring; they are vigorous and practical, and have a somewhat mannish disposition. At menstruation their menstrual blood flows neither too little nor too abundantly.

And because they have thick veins they are very fertile and conceive easily, for their womb and all their inner organs, too, are well developed. They attract men and make men pursue them, and so men love them well. If they want to stay away from men, they can do so without being affected by it badly, though they are slightly affected. However, if they do avoid making love with men they will become difficult and unpleasant in their behaviour. But if they go with men and do not wish to avoid men's love-making, they will be unbridled and over-lascivious, according to men's report. And because they are to some extent mannish on account of vital force [*viriditas*, lit. 'greenness'] within them, a little down sometimes grows on their chin . . .

(*De colerica*) There are other women who have slender flesh but big bones, moderately sized veins and dense red blood. They are pallid in colouring, prudent and benevolent, and men show them reverence and are afraid of them. They suffer much loss of blood in menstruation; their womb is well developed and they are fertile. And men like their conduct, yet flee from them and avoid them to some extent, for they can interest men but not make men desire them. If they do get married, they are chaste, they remain loyal wives and live healthily with their husband; and if they are unmarried, they tend to be ailing – as much because they do not know to what man they might pledge their womanly loyalty as because they lack a husband . . .

(*De melancolica*) But there are other women who have gaunt flesh and thick veins and moderately sized bones; their blood is more lead-coloured than sanguine, and their colouring is as it were blended with grey and black. They are changeable and free-roaming in their thoughts, and wearisomely wasted away in affliction; they also have little power of resistance, so that at times they are worn out by melancholy. They suffer much loss of blood in menstruation, and they are sterile, because they have a weak and fragile womb. So they cannot lodge or retain or warm a man's seed, and thus they are also healthier, stronger and happier without husbands than with them – especially because, if they lie with their husbands, they will tend to feel weak afterwards. But men turn away from them and shun them, because they do not speak to men affectionately, and love them only a little. If for some hour they experience sexual joy, it quickly passes in them. Yet some such women, if they unite with robust and sanguine husbands, can at times, when they reach a fair age, such as fifty, bear at least one child . . . If their menopause comes before the just age, they will sometimes suffer gout or swellings of the legs, or will incur an insanity which their melancholy arouses, or else back-ache or a kidney-ailment . . . If they are not helped in their illness, so that they are not freed from it either by God's help or by medicine, they will quickly die.

Dronke 180–1, 247–9; Kaiser 879

HILDEGARD'S SONGS

Antiphon for God the Father I

O great Father,
Great is our need,
And so we beseech you now
By your Word
Through which you filled us
With what we lacked;
Let it please you now, Father,
– for it is fitting –
To look upon us
In case we fail
And your name is darkened within us,
Which is our help in need.

(6)

Antiphon for God the Father II

O eternal God,
Now let it please you
To burn in that love
So that we become those limbs
Which you made in that same love
When you gave birth to your Son
In the first dawn
Before all creatures,
And look on this need
Which falls upon us.
Take it from us
For the sake of your Son
And lead us into the bliss of salvation.

(7)

Antiphon for the Virgin I

Today, there opens for us
A door once closed,
Which a serpent barred in a woman:
And so there gleams the flower of our Lady,
Brilliant in the dawn.

(11)

Antiphon for the Virgin II

You who are a branch
Thick with leaves,
Who stand in your nobility,
As the dawn breaks,
Rejoice now and be glad,
And deign to free us,
Who are weak,
From evil ways.
Stretch forth your hand,
And raise us on high.

(15)

Alleluia for the Virgin

Alleluia!
O branch Mediatrix,
Your sacred womb
Overcame death
And illumined
All creatures
In the fair flower
Born of the sweetest integrity
Of your sealed chastity.

(18)

Responsory for the Virgin

Sweet branch,
From the stock of Jesse,
How magnificent
That God saw the girl's beauty,
Like an eagle,
Fixing its eye on the sun:

When the highest Father saw
The girl's radiance
And desired his Word
To take flesh in her.

For in the hidden mystery of God,
Her mind was filled with light,
And there emerged from the Virgin
A bright flower,
Wonderfully:

When the highest Father saw
The girl's radiance
And desired his Word
To take flesh in her.

(21)

Antiphon for the Holy Spirit I

The Holy Spirit is life that gives life,
Moving all things.
It is the root in every creature
And purifies all things,
Wiping away sins,
Anointing wounds.
It is radiant life, worthy of praise,
Awakening and enlivening
All things.

(24)

Antiphon for divine love

Love
Gives herself to all things,
Most excellent in the depths,
And above the stars
Cherishing all:
For the High King
She has given
The kiss of peace.

(25)

Antiphon for Saint John the Evangelist

O mirror of the dove
Of form most chaste,
Who saw the hidden wealth
In the spring most pure.

O wonderful flowering
Who never withered and fell:
The All-highest planted you.

O sweet repose
Of the sun's embraces.
You are the Lamb's special child
In the chosen friendship
Of a new race.

(35)

Responsory for Martyrs

You, flowers of the rose,
You are blessed
In the shedding of your blood,
Fragrant in your supreme joy
And moist in the purchase
Which flowed
From the inner mind of the design
Which endures from before
All time:

In him who has no beginning.

Let there be honour in your company,
Who are a channel for the Church,
borne on the tide of your wounds' blood:

In him who has no beginning.

(38)

Antiphon for Saint Disibod

O blessed childhood
Of Disibod the chosen,
So filled with God's Spirit
That you later shed
In the midst of God's marvels,
Holy works,
Like the sweet scent
Of balsam.

(44)

Antiphon for Saint Boniface

O Boniface,
The living light looked upon you,
As on a wise man, who returned
To God the pure streams
That flowed from him,
When you watered the flowers' green.

And so you are a friend of the living God,
A luminous crystal
In the benign intent
Of the righteous ways
In which,
Wise,
You ran.

(51)

Antiphon for Virgins

Faces of beauty,
Beholding God,
Building in the dawn.
Blessed virgins,
How noble you are,
In whom God saw himself
When in you
He gave first sign
Of Heaven's beauty.
You are a most exquisite garden,
Scented with all splendour.

(55)

Responsory for Virgins

Green life, most noble,
Rooted in the sun,
Bright and serene,
You shine in a sphere
Beyond all earthly excellence.

You are enfolded
In the embrace of
Divine ministries.

You blush like the dawn,
And like the sun's flame,
You burn.

(56)

Antiphon for St Ursula

Blood's crimson
Flowing from a height
Touched by God:
You are a blossom
Which the winter
Of the serpent's breath
Did not harm.

(61)

HILDEGARD'S LETTERS

Letter to Bernard of Clairvaux

This is the earliest of Hildegard's letters which we possess, and it was sent in 1147. Since receiving God's command in 1141 to write her visions down, Hildegard had suffered from acute uncertainty. She turned therefore for confirmation of her calling to Bernard, who was currently preaching the Second Crusade and who was one of the most authoritative men in Europe. In his reply to her, Bernard would offer Hildegard support and encouragement.

Reverend Father Bernard, the great honours you have attained through the power of God are a source of wonder; you are truly to be feared by the lawless folly of this world. Under the banner of the Holy Cross, you draw men in exalted devotion, burning with love for the Son of God, to do battle in Christ's army against the savagery of the heathens. I beg you, Father, through the living God, to listen to me as I question you. I am greatly troubled by this vision which has appeared to me through the inspiration of divine mystery. I have never seen it with the outer eyes of the flesh. Wretched as I am (and more than wretched in bearing the name of woman) I have seen, ever since I was a child, great miracles, which my tongue could not utter had the Spirit of God not shown me them so that I might believe. Most true and gentle Father, answer in your goodness, your unworthy maidservant. For never, since I was a child, have I lived an hour free from care. Provide your servant-girl with comfort from your heart.

For in the text, I understand the inner meaning of the exposition of the Psalms and Gospels and the other books which are shown to me by this vision. The vision touches my heart and soul like a burning flame, showing me these depths of interpretation. Yet it does not show me writings in the German tongue – these I do not understand. I only know how to read the words as a single unit – I cannot pull the text apart for analysis.

So tell me please what all of this seems to you to signify – for I am someone untaught by any schooling in external matters (though I have been taught within, in my soul), so that I speak, as though in doubt. But having heard of your wisdom and your holiness, I know that I will be comforted. For I have not dared to tell these things to anyone (since I have heard that there are many schisms in the world) except to a certain monk whose conduct in the community won my approval. To him I revealed all my secrets and he did indeed reassure me that these were great and worthy of reverence. Father, for the love of God, I want you to comfort me, and I will be certain.

Two years ago, I saw you in this vision as one who looked into the sun without being frightened – a truly brave man. And I wept because I blush so deeply and am so timorous.

Noble and most gentle Father, I depend upon your soul. Make it clear to me, if you will, through this exchange, whether I should say these things in the open or maintain my silence. For it costs me great pains to say what I have seen and heard in this vision. Yet, because I have kept silent, I have been laid out by this vision all this time on my bed, in great sickness, unable even to lift myself up. And so I wail before you, in sorrow. For I am prone to the motion of the wine-press lever in my nature – the nature sprung from the root that rose from the Devil's promptings, which entered into Adam, and made him an outcast in an alien world. But now, rising up, I run to you. I tell you: You are not moved by that lever but are always lifting it up. You are a vanquisher in your soul, raising not just yourself, but the world as well, towards salvation.

You are also the eagle looking at the sun. I beg you, through the serenity of the Father and through his wondrous Word, through the sweet tears of remorse, the Spirit of truthfulness, the holy sound with which all creation echoes, and that very

Word from which the world was born, and through the loftiness of the Father who, in sweet greening, sent the Word into the Virgin's womb, from which it sucked flesh, just as honey is walled around by the comb. And may that very sound, the power of the Father, fall into your heart, and lift up your mind so that you are not numbed when you receive my words, so long as you seek all things from God, or from man, or from the mystery itself, until you pass through the opening in your soul, to know all these things in God.

Farewell. Be strong in your soul and firm in God's struggle. Amen.

Letter to Richardis of Stade

Richardis was a nun in the women's cloister at Disibodenberg and then at Rupertsberg. She collaborated closely with Hildegard in the production of her visionary writings. In 1151, shortly after their arrival at Rupertsberg, Richardis was appointed abbess of a Benedictine community at Bassum in the north of Germany. Hildegard opposed her appointment but was unable to prevent Richardis from leaving. Richardis died shortly after receiving Hildegard's letter.

Daughter, hear me, your mother in the spirit, saying to you: My grief rises up. Grief kills the great trust and solace that I found in a human being. From now on I shall say: 'It is good to set one's hope in the Lord, better than to set it in the world's mighty ones.' That is, man ought to look to the one on high, the living one, quite unshaded by any love or feeble trust such as the dark sublunary air offers for a brief time. One who beholds God thus raises the eyes like an eagle to the sun. And because of this one should not look to a high personage, who fails as flowers fall.

I fell short of this, because of love for a noble person. Now I tell you, whenever I have sinned in this way, God has made that sin clear to me in some experiences of anguish or of pain –

and this has now happened on account of you, as you yourself know.

Now, again, I say: Woe is me, your mother, woe is me, daughter – why have you abandoned me like an orphan? I loved the nobility of your conduct, your wisdom and chastity, your soul and the whole of your life, so much that many said: What are you doing?

Now let all who have a sorrow like my sorrow mourn with me – all who have ever, in the love of God, had such high love in heart and mind for a human being as I for you – for one snatched away from them in a single moment, as you were from me.

But may the angel of God precede you, and the Son of God protect you, and his mother guard you. Be mindful of your poor mother Hildegard, that your happiness may not fail.

Letter to Elisabeth of Schönau

Elisabeth was a Benedictine nun at the convent of Schönau near St Goarshausen on the Rhine. She was a younger woman than Hildegard but similarly gifted as a visionary, although her visions differ in kind. On the advice of her brother, she committed them to writing (three books still survive), becoming both famous and the object of unwelcome rumour. She wrote to Hildegard, describing the manner of her visions in full and seeking to redress the unfounded rumours against her. This is Hildegard's reply.

I am a mere poor woman; a vessel of clay. What I say comes not from me but from the clear light: man is a vessel which God fashioned for himself, and filled with his inspiration, so that, in him, he could bring his works to perfection. For God does not work as man does, but all things were perfected in obedience to his command. Vegetation, woods and trees appeared; the sun, the moon and the stars came forth to render service; the waters produced fish and birds of the air; and cattle and wild beasts sprang up; and they all serve man, just as God intended them to. But man alone did not recognize him. For when God provided man with great knowledge, man puffed himself up in his mind and thus alienated himself from God. God had considered that in man, of all creatures, he would perfect his works. But the old deceiver tricked him with the seductive whisper of subversion and infected him with the vice of disobedience, so that he sought more than was right.

Ah! What woe! Then all the elements entangled themselves in an alternation of light and darkness, just as man did in transgressing God's precepts. But God nurtured some mortals, so that man should not be held in universal derision. Abel was a good man; but Cain was a murderer. And many saw in light the mysteries of God; but others committed many sins until the coming of the time when the Word of God began to shine, as was said: 'More beautiful than the sons of men'.

Then the sun of Justice came out and illuminated mortals in faith and action with good works, just as the dawn appears first and the hours of the day follow until the approach of night. So, daughter Elisabeth, the world is changed. For now the world has exhausted all the greenness of virtues – at dawn, at the first, the third, and, above all, the sixth hour of the day. And so, in this time, it is necessary for God to bedew some mortals, lest his instruments fall idle. Listen, my troubled daughter, for the ambitious promptings of the old serpent cause some vexation even to those whom God's inspiration has filled in this way. For when the serpent sees a pretty jewel, he hisses, at once, and says, 'What is this?' And he torments it with the many afflictions of a mind that burns with desire to fly above the clouds (just as he himself has done) as though mortals were gods.

Now listen again: Those who desire to bring the works of God to perfection should pay attention; for, being mortals, they are vessels of clay. And let them always have regard to what they are, and what they will be, and leave the things of heaven to him who is heavenly. For they themselves are outcasts, knowing nothing of the things of heaven, but merely hymning the mysteries of God, just as a trumpet emits sounds but does not make them; for someone else breathes into it to produce the sound.

But let them, too, put on the armour of faith, since they are gentle and mild, poor and wretched (just as that lamb was, whose trumpet-sound they are) and since they have the innocent natures of children. For God always scourges those who play upon his trumpet, while seeing to it that the vessel of clay does not break, but gives him pleasure.

O daughter, may God make you a mirror of life. As for me, I lie in the faint-heartedness of fear, from time to time sounding a little, from the living light, like the small sound of the trumpet. And so may God help me to remain in his service.

Letter to Bishop Eberhard II of Bamberg

Eberhard was consecrated bishop by Pope Eugenius III in 1146. He proved himself an excellent bishop, mediating between the interests of Pope and Emperor in troubled times. He was a man of holy reputation, and a fine theologian. He wrote to Hildegard, reminding her of the theological task which he had set her when they met regarding the proposition that 'Eternity lives in the Father; identity in the Son and the unity of eternity and identity in the Holy Spirit'. This is Hildegard's reply.

The Father is brightness, and that brightness has brilliance and that brilliance has fire, and they are one. Those who do not grasp this in faith do not see God because they try to separate from him what he is – for God is not to be divided. Even the works which God has fashioned lose the original signification that is proper to their names, when man divides them. This brightness is the Father's love. All things are born from it and it surrounds all things, because they derive from its power.

The Father arranges, but the Son performs. For the Father has ordained all things in himself, and the Son has carried them out. The light is part of the light which was there in the beginning, before time and in eternity, and this is the Son who shines from the Father – the Son through whom all creatures were made. And the Son, who had never before appeared in bodily form, even put on the outer form of man, whom he had fashioned from mud. In this way, God saw all the works before him as light, and when he said, 'Let there be', each thing took on an outer form according to its type.

In the Holy Spirit there is the union of eternity and identity. The Holy Spirit is like a fire – but not an extinguishable fire, at one moment visibly ablaze, at another, quenched. For the Holy Spirit produces eternity and identity, and joins them so that they are one, just as someone binds together a bundle. For if a bundle were not bound together, it would not be a bundle but would be scattered. In the same way, too, a blacksmith joins two pieces of metal into one by means of fire. So it is that the Holy Spirit is like a whirling sword being brandished on all sides. It reveals eternity, it makes identity burn bright, so that they are one. The Holy Spirit is the fire and life in that eternity and identity, because God is alive. For the sun is bright and its light blazes and in it burns the fire that illuminates all the world; and yet it appears as a single entity.

Anything in which there is no force is dead, just as the wood torn from the tree is dry because it has no power of greening. For the Holy Spirit is the strengthener and the quickener. Eternity would not be eternity without the Holy Spirit. And identity would not be identity without the Holy Spirit. For the Holy Spirit is in them both and together with them in Godhead is the one God.

Letter to Pope Anastasius IV

Following Eugenius, Anastasius IV reigned briefly as Pope between 12 July, 1153, and 3 December, 1154. Although an upright figure himself, he won a reputation for tolerating lesser men in positions of influence. Hildegard shows no mercy to him on account of his high position as leader of the Church.

So it is, O man, that you who sit in the chief seat of the Lord, hold him in contempt when you embrace evil, since you do not reject it but kiss it, by silently tolerating it in depraved men. And so the whole earth is disordered by a great succession of heresies; for man loves what God has destroyed. And you, Rome, like a man lying at the point of death, will be so confounded that the strength of your feet, on which up till now you have stood, will ebb away. For you love the King's daughter Justice, not with a burning love, but as though in the numbness of sleep; so that you drive her from you. But she herself will flee from you if you do not call her back.

But the high mountains will still hold out to you the jawbone of assistance. They will lift you up, supporting you with the massive timbers of tall trees, so that you will not be despoiled completely of all your honour – the glory of your betrothal to Christ. You will keep some wings to adorn you, until the snow of manifold mockeries arrives, producing much folly. Beware, therefore, of wanting to associate yourself with the ways of the pagans, lest you fall.

Now listen to him who lives and will not be destroyed. The world at this time is steeped in wantonness; after this, it will be in sadness; then in terror, so that people will not be concerned if they are killed. In between these phases, there will be periods of impudence, periods of remorse, and times when various injustices will thunder and blaze like lightning. For the eye steals, the nose ravishes, the mouth kills. But the heart will save, when the dawn will appear with the splendour of the first sunrise. But what follows in the new desire, in the new zeal, is beyond utterance.

Letter to her Community

Here Hildegard is writing to her nuns at Rupertsberg shortly after the resolution of difficulties concerning the establishment of the convent.

But O, what mighty sorrow these daughters of mine will feel after the death of their mother, since her words will rise no longer. And so in their grief and mourning, through the many seasons of their tears, they will cry, 'Alas! alas! how happily we would suck at our mother's breasts if only we had her with us now!' For this reason, Daughters of God, I urge you as your mother, (as I have urged you from my youth) to keep love amongst you, so that you may be a light renowned with the angels, for your kindness, and mighty in your powers, just as your Father Benedict taught you. The Holy Spirit urges its gifts upon you; for after my death, you will hear my voice no longer.

Yet never let my voice, which has sounded so often amongst you in love, be drawn into oblivion. My daughters now are glowing red in their hearts because of the sorrow they feel for their mother. They are panting and sighing for the things of heaven. Afterwards, they will shine, through the grace of God, with a dazzling red light. They will become the bravest soldiers in his house. If anyone should wish to incite, in this throng of my daughters, dissension from the spiritual rule or schism in this community, may the gift of the Holy Spirit remove such a wish from that person's heart. But if, in contempt of God, they should commit this deed, may the hand of the Lord strike them down in front of all the people, because they deserve to be confounded.

For this reason, my daughters, dwell in that place, where you have chosen to be soldiers of God, with all your steadfastness and devotion, so that in it you may obtain the rewards of heaven.

Letter to the monks of St Eucharius

This is one of many letters Hildegard wrote in which she exhorts male religious to higher spiritual standards. The community concerned was an important and ancient foundation in Trier with which she was connected. The community still exists today and is known as the Abbey of St Matthias.

But now the living light says to the sons of that throng: You are the walls of the Temple; for the primitive Church set you in place. So shun vanity and pride and avoid the whirlwind of unrest. Look at these things now with living eyes; and hear these words by listening with your inner ears. I do not see your community being scattered, although it will feel the smart of many whips. Live therefore and be vigilant in God. For in the true vision, I saw some in that congregation who have the red glow of the dawn, who glitter like sapphire, who shine like the light of the stars. For those who glow red like the dawn, hold God in fear and willingly observe, on his account, the precepts of the community Rule; although, due to the flesh, they seem now and then to stray from the path, like a sacrificial beast being led to the slaughter.

But those who shine like the sapphire, love God, and hence do not commit grave sins, although they do sin; and it is their custom to chastise themselves readily for their transgressions. But those who shine like the light of the stars are full of good-will and consequently do not quarrel with others, but they hold in check the petulance of childish natures and willingly abstain from serious sins, considering them hateful. And I have seen others enveloped in the blackness of acrid smoke, because of their habitually foul behaviour. Some of these are acrid because of the peculiar nature of their minds. For they love riches, and consequently do not love the spiritual way of life.

Letter to Abbess Hazzecha of Krauftal

Hildegard had visited the Benedictine community at Krauftal in 1160 and had continued to correspond with Hazzecha, who sought to escape from her responsibilities as abbess by becoming a hermit, or by going on pilgrimage. Hildegard advised Hazzecha to persevere in the task allotted to her. The 'lady abbess H' addressed in this letter is almost certainly Hazzecha.

To the lady abbess H, Hildegard. In true vision I saw and heard these words:

Daughter of God, you that in God's love call me – poor little creature – mother, learn to have discretion, which, in heavenly things and earthly, is the mother of us all, since by this the soul is directed, and the body nurtured in appropriate restraint. A person who, amid sighs of repentance, remembers sins committed – thinking, speaking, acting at the devil's prompting – should embrace her mother, discretion, and be submissive to her, and in true humility and obedience should correct her sins, in the way that her teachers advise. Indeed, as the fruit of the earth is harmed by a freak rainstorm, and as from untilled earth sprout no true fruits, but useless weeds, so a person who toils more than her body can bear is rendered useless in her spirit by ill-judged toil and ill-judged abstinence.

When the blackest of birds – the devil – senses that someone wants to banish illicit longings and cease from sins, it curls itself into the fasting, prayers and abstinence of that person, like a viper into its den; suggestively it says to her: 'Your sins can't be wiped out unless you trample down your body with tears and grief, and with such immense labours that it withers totally.' So, living hopeless and joyless, that person's senses often fail, she is fettered by grievous sickness, and thus, despoiled of the quality of holiness by the devil's deceit, she leaves what she began without discretion unfinished, and in this way her last condition will be worse than the earlier one.

Also, let one who is bound in obedience, in accord with Christ's example, take utmost care not to choose something in a self-willed way, trusting more in herself than in the good advice of others – lest she be overcome by the pride that tumbled from heaven, by wanting to be better than others who are good, reckoning that to be good and holy which is decided by herself. For of herself she can know this, that she should not acquiesce in her own will, since she exists in two natures – body and soul – and these discord, as what pleases the one displeases the other. This being so in human beings, how can they, their soul unharmed, consent to their own will, which belongs to the body? But the person who, for fear and love of God, devises her own will, and submits herself to the precepts, instruction and rule of her teachers, offering example to others in true humility of good works – she makes herself a living tabernacle in the heavenly Jerusalem; the Holy Spirit rests on her.

Dearest daughter, I cannot see that it will help you and your two dependants to seek a forest or a recluse's cell or a pilgrimage to Rome, since you are already marked with the seal of Christ, with which you journey to the heavenly Jerusalem. For if you embark on a greater effort than you can endure, through the devil's deceit – as I said – you will fall.

In the love of Christ, too, I tell you that it is not my wont to speak of the end or the achievements of people, or of what will befall them; but the things I am taught by the Holy Spirit in the vision of my soul – though I am untaught – these I speak and write. As for the men whom you commended to me, in my prayers I gladly commend them to the grace of God. I'll also gladly pray to God for you, that he free you from everything that is ill-suited to you, and that he guard you from future ills.

And may you perfect the efforts of holy works with such blessed discretion that, strengthened by the radiance of pure holiness and kindled by the ardour of true love of God, you may attain the supreme bliss. May you live in it forever.

Letter to an abbot

Hildegard uses her medical analysis of people's characters to console a friend, an unknown abbot who is evidently experiencing some difficulties with his community.

The secret mysteries of God cannot be comprehended or known by anything that has its source through the Beginning. And yet all his judgements are just, because there is no emptiness in him: he is as he was and is. But even as man consists of elements, and the elements are conjoined, and none is of any avail of itself without another, so too the modes of behaviour of men are unequal, even though they arise from one and the same breath of life.

There are four modes of behaviour among men: some are hard, some airy, some stormy, some fiery.

One who has the hard mode is sharp in everything, and in none of his affairs does he heed anyone else, but reckons all that is his for himself alone, and takes pleasure in that.

And as for one who has the airy mode, his mind is always wavering; and yet he fears God and restrains himself as regards sinning, because he is not pleased with what he does.

Those who have the stormy mode are not wise, but compound all they do with foolishness; they are not improved by words of wisdom, but shudder at them indignantly.

And those who have the fiery mode aspire to everything worldly and alienate themselves from spiritual people; they shun peace and, wherever they see it, strike at it with some worldly ambition . . .

But God gathers to himself some of all those who have such

modes of behaviour – when, growing aware, they turn what goes against their souls' salvation back towards God: those who at last fear him, as happened in the case of Saul and many others.

Letter to King Henry II of England

Henry II was crowned King of England in 1154. He greatly admired the Emperor, Barbarossa, and a marriage was planned between the babies of the two royal houses, which Henry cancelled when his future son-in-law was passed over in the imperial succession. King Henry supported the antipope, while the English bishops, Thomas à Becket among them, supported Pope Alexander. Henry became Thomas's enemy, but did penance after his murder at Canterbury in 1170. The Archbishop was canonized three years later.

To a certain man who holds a certain office, the Lord says: 'Yours are the gifts of giving: it is by ruling and defending, protecting and providing, that you may reach heaven.' But a bird, as black as can be, comes to you from the North and says: 'You have the power to do whatever you want. So do this and do that; make this excuse and that excuse. It does not profit you to have regard for Justice; for if you are always attentive to her, you will not be a master but a slave.'

Yet you should not listen to the thief who gives you this advice; the thief who, in your infancy, when you had become, from ashes, a thing of beauty, after receiving the breath of life, stripped you of great glory. Look, instead, more attentively upon your Father who made you. For your mind is well-disposed, so that you readily do good, except when the foul habits of others overwhelm you and you become entangled in them for a time. Shun this, with all your might, beloved son of God, and call upon your Father, since willingly he stretches out his hand to help you. Now live forever and remain in eternal happiness.

Letter to Werner of Kirchheim

Hildegard's last preaching tour took her to Swabia in 1170 or 1171, where she visited Kirchheim and spoke to a community of priests. Their leader, Werner of Kirchheim, wrote to Hildegard requesting a copy of her address. This is part of her reply.

In the year of our Lord's incarnation, 1170, I had been lying on my sick-bed for a long time, when I saw (fully conscious in body and in mind) a most beautiful image. It took the form of a woman, and so exceptional was her sweetness and so rich in delights her beauty, that the human mind was powerless to comprehend her. She stretched in height from earth to heaven. Her face shone with exceeding brightness and her gaze was fixed on heaven. She was dressed in a dazzling robe of white silk and draped in a cloak, adorned with stones of great price – with emerald, with sapphire and with pearls, having about her feet shoes of onyx.

But her face was stained with dust and her robe was ripped down the right side and her cloak had lost its sheen of beauty and her shoes had been blackened. And she herself, in a voice loud with sorrow, was calling to the heights of heaven, saying, 'Hear, heaven, how my face is sullied; mourn, earth, that my robe is torn; tremble, abyss, because my shoes are blackened. "Foxes have lairs and the birds of the air have nests", but I have no helper and no comforter, no staff to lean on for support.' And again she began to speak:

'I lay hidden in the heart of the Father until the Son of Man, who was conceived and born in virginity, poured out his blood. With that same blood, he made me his betrothed and furnished me with a dowry, so that, in a pure and simple regeneration of spirit and water, I might give new life to those constrained and tainted by the serpent's venom.

'But my nurturers, the priests – who ought to make my face glow red like the dawn, my robe gleam like lightning, my cloak sparkle like precious stones and my shoes glisten like whiteness itself – have strewn my face with dust, and torn my robe, and made my cloak a thing of shadows; my shoes they have blackened utterly. The very people who ought to adorn me in every part, have left me destitute in all these respects.

'For they sully my face by handling and receiving the body and blood of my Bridegroom, despite the impurity of their lascivious habits, the vast filth of their fornications and adulteries and the wicked plunder of their avarice, in which they sell and buy all manner of improper things; and they roll around in such a quantity of muck, that it is as if a little child were placed in the mire at the feet of pigs.

'For just as man became flesh and blood, when God made him from the earth's mud and breathed into his face the breath of life; so too, while the priest's words are invoking divinity, that same power of God changes the offering of bread and wine and water on the altar into the true flesh and true blood of Christ, my Bridegroom. But because of the blindness which afflicted man at Adam's fall, man is unable to see with the eyes of the flesh. For my Bridegroom's wounds, where the nails were driven in, remain fresh and open as long as the wounds of men's sins continue to gape. The priests (who ought to make me radiantly pure, by serving me in radiant purity) infect these same wounds of Christ's, as they scurry from church to church in their excessive avarice.

'They also tear my robe, since they are violators of the law, the gospel and their own priesthood; and they darken my cloak by neglecting, in every way, the rules which they are meant to uphold; nor do they fulfil them (in good intentions or in actual practice) through abstinence (as symbolized by the emerald) or in the distribution of alms (as symbolized by the sapphire), nor through the other good and just works with which God is honoured (as symbolized by the other types of jewels).

'But my shoes, too, are blackened on the tops, since the priests do not keep to the straight paths of justice, which are hard and rugged, or set good examples to those beneath them; although, on the underside of my shoes (as in my inner self), I find, in some, the radiance of truth.'

Letter to Guibert of Gembloux

Here Hildegard is writing to the man who was to become her secretary in reply to his request for a detailed description of how she came to receive her visions. This letter gives us the most profound insight into the nature of Hildegard's visions and of her calling.

These words come not from me nor from any other mortal: but I present them as I received them in a vision from above. O servant of God, through the mirror of faith in which you look in order to know God; O son of God, through the fashioning of man in whom God wrought and expressed his miracles (for just as a mirror – in which all manner of things are seen – is placed in its frame, so too, the rational soul is inserted in the body, as though in a vessel of clay; so that, through it, the body may be guided in its mode of living and the heavenly soul may be contemplated through faith), listen to what the unfailing light says:

Man is both of heaven and of earth – through the good understanding of his rational soul, he is heavenly; and through his evil understanding, he is frail and full of shadows; and the more he identifies himself with good things, the more completely he loves God. For if he saw his face in the mirror, befouled and sprinkled with dust, he would be anxious to wipe it clean. So that even if he understands that he has sinned and been entangled in a variety of vanities, let him sigh; since he knows, in his good understanding, that he has been defiled; and let him lament with the psalmist, saying, 'O wretched daughter of Babylon, blessed is the man who will pay you back the retribution you have bestowed on us; blessed he, who will seize your children and dash them against the rock'.

Which is to say: man's desire was confounded through the serpent's venom. For in itself it is poor and destitute, since in speculative knowledge it lacks an honourable reputation, for it does not desire to seek the glory of eternal life, of which it has a foretaste through its good knowledge. But blessed is he who will grasp the fact that he lives from God, and whose understanding shows him that God made him and redeemed him and who, because of this freedom which God gave him, obliterates the evil habit of his sins, and hurls against that rock (which is the chief support of blessedness), all the misery and poverty he has in heavenly riches. For when man recognizes the foul rottenness in himself, and cannot restrain himself by any means from tasting sin, then the pitch-black birds defile him utterly.

And although man knows that he exists in this way and that he lives in the infinite life, he is nevertheless unable to prevent himself from sinning frequently. And so, how full of wonder and of sorrow is the cry, that God made such vessels of clay, all starry with his miracles, when the vessels themselves could not forsake sin, unless through the grace of God it was forbidden them. Not even Peter was immune; Peter who fervently vowed that he would never deny the Son of God. Nor were many other holy men, who fell in their sins, but afterwards became more useful and more excellent than they would have been had they not fallen.

O faithful servant, I, a poor little figure of a woman, tell you these words again in a true vision. Even if it pleased God to lift up my body in this vision in the same way as my soul, fear would still not retreat from my mind and heart, because, although I have been enclosed since I was a child, I know that I am human. Many wise men have been so inspired by miracles that they have revealed a great many mysteries, but because of vanity they have credited these to themselves and so have fallen. But those who, in the soaring of their souls, have drunk their wisdom from God and reckoned themselves as nothing, these have become the pillars of heaven. Such was the case with Paul who surpassed the other disciples in his preaching and yet reckoned himself as nothing. John the Evangelist, too, was full of gentle humility, so that he drank deeply of the Godhead.

And how could I, a poor little woman, not know what I am? God works where he wills, for the glory of his name, and not for that of mortals. Indeed, I have always trembled with fear, since I am not confident of any ability in myself; but I hold out my hands to God, so that I might be supported by him, like a feather which has no weight or strength and which flies on the wind. And I cannot fully understand what I see while I remain in the service of the body and the invisible soul, since human beings are deficient in both these respects.

But ever since I was a child (when I was not yet strengthened in my bones and nerves and veins) I have always seen this vision in my soul, right up to the present time, when I am over seventy, and my soul, just as God willed, climbs in this vision, through the changes of atmosphere, to the top of the firmament and spreads itself out amongst different peoples, although they are a long way away from me in distant regions and places. And since I see these things in this way in my soul, I therefore also see them according to the changing of the clouds and of other creatures. But I do not hear these things with my outer ears, nor do I perceive them with the rational parts of my mind, nor with any combination of my five senses; but only in my soul, with my outer eyes open, so that I never suffer in them any unconsciousness induced by ecstasy, but I see them when I am awake, by day and by night. And I am constantly constrained by my infirmities, and many times I have been so enveloped by grave afflictions that they threatened to set death upon me, but up till now, God has sustained me.

The light which I see is not confined to one place, but it is far, far brighter than a cloud which carries the sun; nor can I gauge its height or length or breadth, and it is known to me by the name of the 'reflection of the living light'. And just as the sun, the moon and the stars appear in the waters, so the Scriptures, sermons and virtues and certain works that humans have wrought, shine on me brightly in this light.

Whatever I see or learn in this vision, I hold in my memory for a long time; so that when I recall what I have seen and heard, I simultaneously see and hear and understand and, as it were, learn in this moment, what I understand. But what I do not see, I do not understand, because I am unlearned. And what I write in the vision, I see and hear; nor do I put down words other than those I hear in the vision, and I present them in Latin, unpolished, just as I hear them in the vision. For I am not taught in this vision to write as the philosophers write; and the words in this vision are not like those which sound from the mouth of man, but like a trembling flame, or like a cloud stirred by the clear air.

I also have no means of knowing the form of this light, in the same way that I cannot look directly at the ball of the sun. In the same light I sometimes (but infrequently) see another light which is known to me by the name of the living light – but when and how I see it, I cannot tell. And while I am looking at it, all sorrow and all perplexity are drained from me, so that I seem then to have the character of an innocent girl and not that of a little old woman.

Yet besides the chronic sickness which I suffer, I find it wearying sometimes to relate the words and visions which are shown to me there. But when my soul experiences the sight of these things, I am transformed into another character, because, as I said, I consign to oblivion all sadness and distress. And what I see and hear in this same vision, my soul drinks as though from a spring; but the spring remains full and undepleted. But at no hour is my soul without the light I spoke of, which is called 'the reflection of the living light'. I see it as though I were in a shining cloud, looking at a firmament without stars; and in it I see the things of which I often speak and which I give in answer to those who ask about the shining of the living light.

But in these two respects – in my body and my soul – I do not know myself and I reckon myself as nothing: and I rely on the living God and I leave all these things to him, so that he who has no beginning and no end may, in all these things, keep me safe from evil. So you who seek these words, and all of those who desire to hear these things in faith, pray for me, that I may continue in the service of God.

Letter to Abbot Ludwig of St Eucharius

Ludwig became abbot of the Benedictine monastery of St Eucharius in Trier (which later changed its name to St Matthias) in 1168. Hildegard had visited the monastery in 1160 and had maintained close links with the community. When her secretary Volmar died in 1173 it was to Ludwig that Hildegard entrusted the text of her greatest visionary work, The Book of Divine Works. *The following letter was probably a covering note sent with the manuscript.*

The sun arises at dawn and, from the place where it is set, perfuses all the clouds with its brightness by beholding them, and rules and lights up all creatures by its ardour, running its course to twilight: in the same way God has made the whole of creation – which is man – and then has vivified and lit it with the breath of life.

For as the earliest dawn rises with damp cold and changing cloud-shapes, so man in his childhood has damp coldness, since his flesh is still growing and his bones are not yet filled with marrow, nor is his blood yet sparkling in full redness. But, as the third hour of the day begins to grow hot in the sun's course, so he too, chewing different foods, acquires their taste, and at the same time learns to walk. When childhood is over, man in youth becomes daring, joyful and serene, making his own plans for what he would like to begin, so that if, turning to the right side, he chooses the good in the sun's light, he will become fruitful in good deeds; but if, pursuing evil, he inclines down to the left side, he will grow black and most foul in sin. But when, accomplishing his course of action, he arrives at the ninth hour, he will falter and dry up in flesh and marrow, and in the other forces with which he advanced as he grew. So too the highest craftsman has drawn up the ages of the world, ordered in time from dawn to twilight.

But you, father, who are so named after the Father, reflect on how you began, and how you proceeded in life: for in your childhood you were foolish, and in youth you were filled with joyous assurance. Meanwhile you have embarked on an adventure of the unicorn – unknown to you in your youth – and this indeed was my writing, which often carries echoes of the mortal dress of the Son of God, who, loving a maidenly nature, resting in it like the unicorn in the maiden's lap, gathered the whole Church to himself with the sweetest sound of fairest believing.

Remember too, loyal father, what you often used to hear for a poor little womanly creature soft in form, about that dress of the Son of God; and, because my helper has been taken away by the highest Judge, I now am entrusting what I have written to you, asking imploringly that you preserve it carefully, and look over it, correcting it lovingly, that your name too may be written in the book of life, imitating the blessed Gregory in this, who, despite the burden of his Roman episcopate, never ceased composing, impelled by the lute-like sound of the infusion of the Holy Spirit.

Put on celestial armour like a noble knight, washing away the deeds of foolishness of your youth, and toil strenuously in the noonday in the angelic robe of your monk's habit, before the day declines, so that you may be welcomed joyously in the heavenly tents into the angels' company.

Letter to the Mainz prelates

In 1178 Hildegard agreed to allow a nobleman who had been excom-municated, but subsequently reconciled to the Church, to be buried on consecrated ground at the Rupertsberg. The Mainz clergy disputed the fact that the man had made his peace with the Church and ordered that his body be exhumed. When Hildegard refused to comply with their request she and her community were placed under an interdict. They were forbidden to hear the Mass, receive the Eucharist or sing the divine office. In the following letter Hildegard explains her actions and indicates her belief that the prelates are wrong in their judgement, particularly in forbidding the nuns to use music in their worship.

In the vision that was fixed within my soul, by God the craftsman, before I came forth in my birth, I was compelled to write this, on account of the fetter by which we have been bound by our superiors, because of a dead man who, at the direction of his priest, was buried without calumny in our midst. When, a few days after his burial, we were ordered by our superiors to fling him out of the cemetery, I, seized with no little terror at this order, looked to the true light, as is my wont. And, my eyes wakeful, I saw in my soul that, if we followed their command and exposed the corpse, such an expulsion would threaten our home with great danger, like a vast black-ness – it would envelop us like a dark cloud that looms before tempests and thunderstorms . . .

So we did not dare expose him . . . not at all because we make light of the advice of honourable men or of our prelates' command, but lest we seem to injure Christ's sacraments – with which the man was blessed while still alive – by women's savagery. Yet, so as not to be wholly disobedient, we have till now ceased singing the songs of divine praises, in accordance with the interdict, and have abstained from partaking of the body of the Lord . . .

While I and all my sisters were afflicted with great bitterness through this, and oppressed by a huge sadness . . . I heard in my vision that I was guilty in that I had not come with all humility and devotion before my superiors, to ask their leave to receive communion, most of all since we were not at fault in accepting the body of that man.

I also beheld something about the fact that, obeying you, we have till now ceased to celebrate the divine office in song, reading it only in a low voice: I heard a voice from the living light tell of the diverse kinds of praises, of which David says in the Psalms: 'Praise him in the call of the trumpet, praise him on psaltery and lute, praise him on the tambour and in dancing, praise him on strings and on organ, praise him on resonant cymbals, praise him on cymbals of jubilation – let every spirit praise the Lord!'

In these words outer realities teach us about inner ones – namely how, in accordance with the material composition and quality of instruments, we can best transform and shape the performance of our inner being towards praises of the Creator. If we strive for this lovingly, we recall how man sought the voice of the living spirit, which Adam lost through disobedience – he who, still innocent before his fault, had no little kinship with the sounds of the angels' praises . . .

But in order that mankind should recall that divine sweetness and praise by which, with the angels, Adam was made jubilant in God before he fell, instead of recalling Adam in his banishment, and that mankind too might be stirred to that sweet praise, the holy prophets – taught by the same spirit, which they had received – not only composed psalms and canticles, to be sung to kindle the devotion of listeners; but also they invented musical instruments of diverse kinds with this in view, by which the songs could be expressed in multitudinous sounds, so that listeners, aroused and made adept outwardly, might be nurtured within by the forms and qualities of the instruments, as by the meaning of the words performed with them.

Eager and wise men imitated the holy prophets, inventing human kinds of harmonized melody (*organa*) by their art, so that they could sing in the delight of their soul; and they adapted their singing to [the notation indicated by] the bending of the finger-joints, as it were recalling that Adam was formed by the finger of God, which is the Holy Spirit, and that in Adam's voice before he fell there was the sound of every harmony and the sweetness of the whole art of music. And if Adam had remained in the condition in which he was formed, human frailty could never endure the power and the resonance of that voice. But when his deceiver, the devil, heard that man had begun to sing through divine inspiration, and that he would be transformed through this to remembering the sweetness of the songs in the heavenly land – seeing the machinations of his cunning going awry, he became so terrified that . . . he has not ceased to trouble or destroy the affirmation and beauty and sweetness of divine praise and of the hymns of the spirit. So you and all prelates must use the greatest vigilance before stopping, by a decree, the mouth of any assembly of people singing to God . . . you must always beware lest in your judgement you are ensnared by Satan, who drew man out of the celestial harmony and the delights of paradise . . .

And because at times, when hearing some melody, a human being often sighs and moans, recalling the nature of the heavenly harmony, the prophet David, subtly contemplating the profound nature of the spirit, and knowing that the human soul is symphonic (*symphonialis*), exhorts us in his psalm to proclaim the Lord on the lute and play for him on the ten-stringed psaltery: he wants to refer his lute, which sounds lower, to the body's control; the psaltery, which sounds higher, to the spirit's striving; its ten chords, to the fulfilment of the Law.

Select Bibliography

HILDEGARD'S WORKS

Scivias

Migne J. P., ed., *Patrologia Latina*, vol. 197 (*PL*).

Führkötter A., and Carlevaris, A., (modern critical edition) *Hildegardis – Scivias. Corpus Christianorum: continuatio mediaeualis*, Brepols, Turnhout, Belgium, vols. 43 & 43A, 1978.

Böckeler, M., (German translation), *Wisse die Wege – Scivias*. St Augustinus Verlag, Berlin, 1928; Otto Müller Verlag, Salzburg, 1954, repr. 1987. Includes colour plates of the illustrated Rupertsberg manuscript of *Scivias*.

Hart, C., and Bishop, T., (English translation), *Hildegard of Bingen: Scivias*. The Classics of Western Spirituality. Paulist Press, New York, 1990. Introduction by Barbara Newman, Preface by Caroline Walker Bynum. Includes black and white illustrations from the Rupertsberg manuscript.

Hozeski, B. (abridged English translation), *Hildegard of Bingen's 'Scivias'*. Bear & Company, Santa Fé, 1986.

Liber vitae meritorum ('The Book of Life's Merits')

Pitra, J. P., *Analecta sacra*, vol. VIII, (Pi).

Schipperges, H., (German translation), *Der Mensch in der Verantwortung – Liber vitae meritorum*. Otto Müller Verlag, Salzburg, 1972.

Liber divinorum operum ('The Book of Divine Works'), (*PL*).

Schipperges, H., (German translation), *Welt und Mensch – Das Buch: De operatione Dei*. Otto Müller Verlag, Salzburg, 1965. Includes colour plates from the illuminated Lucca manuscript of *The Book of Divine Works*.

Fox, M., (ed.), (abridged English translation, including some of Hildegard's letters and songs), *Hildegard of Bingen's Book of Divine Works*, Bear & Company, Santa Fé, 1987.

Liber subtilitarum diversarum naturarum creaturarum:
Liber simplicis medicinae/Physica ('Book of Simple Medicine or Natural History'), (*PL*).

Riether, P., (German translation), *Naturkunde: Das Buch von dem inneren Wesen der verschiedenen Naturen in der Schöpfung – Physica*, Otto Müller Verlag, Salzburg, 1959.

Liber compositae medicinae/Causae et curae ('Book of Compound Medicine or Causes and Cures')

Kaiser, P., *Hildegardis Causae et curae*, Leipzig, 1903.

Schipperges, H., *Heilkunde: Das Buch von dem Grund und Wesen und der Heilung der Krankheiten – Causae et curae*. Otto Müller Verlag, Salzburg, 1957.

Symphonia harmoniae caelestium revelationum ('Symphony of the Harmony of Celestial Revelations'), (Pi).

Barth, P., Ritscher, I., and Schmidt-Görg, J., *Hildegard von Bingen: Lieder*. Otto Müller Verlag, Salzburg, 1969.

Newman, B., (English/Latin critical edition), *Saint Hildegard of Bingen: Symphonia*. Cornell University Press, Ithaca and London, 1988.

Ordo virtutum ('Play of the Virtues'), (Pi).

Dronke, P., (Critical edition) in *Poetic Individuality in the Middle Ages*. Oxford 1970.

Expositio evangeliorum ('Commentary on the Gospels'), (Pi).

Lingua ignota ('Unknown Language'), (*PL*).

Roth, F. W. E., *Die Lieder und die unbekannte Sprache der hl.Hildegardis*. Wiesbaden 1860.

Litterae ignotae ('Unknown Writing'), (Pi).

Explanatio Regulae S. Benedicti ('Commentary on the Rule of St Benedict'), (*PL*).

Explanatio Symboli S. Athanasii ('Commentary on the Athanasian Creed'), (*PL*).

Vita S. Ruperti ('Life of St Rupert'), (*PL*).

Vita S. Disibodi ('Life of St Disibod'), (*PL*).

Epistolae ('Letters'), (Pi, *PL*, Berlin Manuscript Lat. Qu. 674).

Führkötter, A., (German selection with excellent introduction and historical notes), *Hildegard von Bingen: Briefwechsel*. Otto Müller Verlag, Salzburg, 1965.

Dronke, P., (Latin text and English tr. of some letters from the Berlin Manuscript), *Women Writers of the Middle Ages*. Cambridge 1984.

Fox, M., (ed.) (Selected letters in English), *Hildegard of Bingen's Book of Divine Works, with Letters and Songs*. Bear & Company, Santa Fé, 1987.

Solutiones triginta octo quaestionum ('Solutions to Thirty-eight Questions'), (*PL*).

Vita sanctae Hildegardis ('Life of St. Hildegard') by Godfrey and Theodoric, (*PL*).

Führkötter, A., (German translation), *Das Leben der hl. Hildegard von Bingen – Vita S. Hildegardis*. Düsseldorf 1968.

Silvas, A., (English translation), 'Saint Hildegard of Bingen and the *Vita Sanctae Hildegardis*', *Tjurunga: An Australian Benedictine Review* 29 (1985), pp. 4–25; 30 (1986), pp. 63–73; 31 (1986), pp. 32–41; 32 (1987), pp. 46–59.

Vita sanctae Hildegardis by Guibert of Gembloux, (Pi).

Acta Inquisitionis ('Proceedings of the Inquisition'), also called *Protocollum canonisationis*.

Bruder, P., *Analecta Bollandiana*, 2, 1883.

SECONDARY WORKS

Allchin, A. M., 'Julian of Norwich and Hildegard of Bingen', *Mount Carmel*, vol. 37, no. 3, Autumn 1989, Oxford, pp. 128–43.

Bonn, C., *Der Mensch in der Entscheidung: Gedanken zur ganzheitlichen Schau Hildegards von Bingen*. Abtei St Hildegard, Eibingen, 1986.

Brück, Anton, ed., *Hildegard von Bingen, 1179–1979. Festschrift zum 800 Todestag der Heiligen*. Mainz 1979.

Clifford Rose, F., and Gawel, M., *Migraine: The Facts*. Oxford 1981.

Dronke, P., 'The Composition of Hildegard of Bingen's *Symphonia*', *Sacris Erudiri* 19, 1969–70, pp. 381–93.

Dronke, P., *Poetic Individuality in the Middle Ages*. Clarendon Press, Oxford, 1970.

Dronke, P., 'Tradition and Innovation in Medieval Western Colour-Imagery', *Eranos Jahrbuch*, vol. 41, 1972, pp. 51–106.

Dronke, P., 'Problemata Hildegardiana', *Mittellateinisches Jahrbuch 16*, 1981, pp. 97–131.

Dronke, P., *Women Writers of the Middle Ages: A Critical Study of Texts from Perpetua (+ 203) to Marguerite Porete (+ 1310)*. Cambridge University Press, Cambridge, 1984.

Epiney-Burgard, G., and Zum Brunn, E., *Femmes Troubadours de Dieu*. Brepols, Belgium, 1988. English translation, *Women Mystics in Medieval Europe*. Paragon House, New York, 1989.

Flanagan, S., *Hildegard of Bingen: A Visionary Life*. Routledge, London and New York, 1989.

Führkötter, A., *Hildegard von Bingen*. Otto Müller Verlag, Salzburg, 1972.

Führkötter, A., *Hildegard von Bingen: Ruf in die Zeit*. Rheinland Verlag, Cologne, 1985.

Führkötter, A., *Kosmos und Mensch aus der Sicht Hildegards von Bingen*. Gesellschaft für Mittelrheinische Kirchengeschichte, Mainz, 1987.

Gronau, E., *Hildegard von Bingen 1098–1179: Prophetische Lehrerin der Kirche an der Schwelle und am Ende der Neuzeit*. Christiana Verlag, Stein am Rhein, 1985.

Gumley, F., and Redhead, B., *The Christian Centuries*. BBC Books, 1989.

Kraft, K., 'The German Visionary: Hildegard of Bingen', *Medieval Women Writers*, ed. Wilson, K., pp. 109–30. Athens, Georgia, 1984.

Lauter, W., *Hildegard-Bibliographie 1*, Alzey 1970, and 2, Alzey 1984.

Mason-Hill, E., (ed.) *Trotula, Diseases of Women*. Ward Richie Press, 1940.

Newman, B., 'Hildegard of Bingen: Visions and Validation', *Church History 54*, 1985, pp. 163–75.

Newman, B., *Sister of Wisdom: St Hildegard's Theology of the Feminine*. Scolar Press, Berkeley, 1987.

Newman, B., *Saint Hildegard of Bingen Symphonia: A Critical Edition of the 'Symphonia armonie celestium revelationum' [Symphony of the Harmony of Celestial Revelations]*. Cornell University Press, Ithaca and London, 1988.

Pereira, M., 'Maternità e Sessualità femminile in Ildegarda di Bingen: Proposte de Lettura', *Quaderni Storici* 44, 1980, pp. 564–79.

Petroff, E., *Medieval Women's Visionary Literature*. Oxford University Press, Oxford, 1986.

Sacks, O., 'The Visions of Hildegard', *The Man who Mistook his Wife for a Hat*. Picador/Pan, London, 1986.

Schipperges, H., *Hildegard von Bingen: Ein Zeichen für unsere Zeit*. Josef Knecht, Frankfurt, 1981.

Schipperges, H. and Bonn, C., *Hildegard von Bingen und ihre Impulse für die moderne Welt*. Abtei St Hildegard, Eibingen, 1984.

Scholz, B., 'Hildegard von Bingen on the Nature of Woman', *American Benedictine Review* 31, 1984, pp. 361–83.

Schrader, M., and Führkötter, A., *Die Echtheit des Schrifttums der hl. Hildegard von Bingen*. Quellenkritische Untersuchungen, Cologne and Graz, 1956.

Schrader, M., *Die Herkunft der Heiligen Hildegard*. Gesellschaft für Mittelrheinische Kirchengeschichte, Mainz, 1981.

Southern, R. W., *The Making of the Middle Ages*. Century Hutchinson, London, 1967.

Steele, F., *The Life and Visions of St. Hildegarde*. London 1914.

Strehlow, W., and Hertzka, G., *Hildegard of Bingen's Medicine*. Bear & Company, Santa Fé, 1988.

Wolff, R., 'Herrschaft und Dienst in Sprache und Natur' in Brück, ed., (1979), pp. 239–62.

Select Discography

A feather on the breath of God: Sequences and hymns by Abbess Hildegard of Bingen. Gothic Voices, directed by Christopher Page, with Emma Kirkby, Margaret Philpot, and Emily Van Evera. Hyperion A66039, recorded London, September 1981.

Geistliche Musik des Mittelalters und der Renaissance. Instrumentalkreise Helga Weber, directed by Helga Weber, with Almut Teichert-Hailperin. TELDEC 66.22387, recorded in Hamburg, May 1980.

Gesänge der hl. Hildegard von Bingen. Schola der Benediktinerinnenabtei St Hildegard in Eibingen, directed by M. I. Ritscher, OSB. Psallite 242/040 479 PET, recorded in Eibingen, April 1979.

Hildegard von Bingen: Ordo virtutum. Sequentia, directed by Klaus Neumann. Harmonia mundi 20395/96, recorded in France, June 1982.

Hildegard von Bingen: Symphoniae (Geistliche Gesänge). Sequentia, directed by Barbara Thornton. Harmonia mundi IC 067-19 9976 I, recorded in Germany, June 1983.